"A new window on the much-neglected invisible dimension of our humanity. Great reading."
— Wayne W. Dyer, author of *The Power of Intention*

"Offers writers an informative, personal conversation on the intricacies of getting the heart down on the page."
— Christina Baldwin, author of *Storycatcher*

"Describes what each of us can do to remove the blocks to our own creativity and thus more fully express our essential being."
— Shakti Gawain, author of *Creative Visualization*

"Combines insight, experience, and ancient wisdom. Not only worth reading but referencing and studying."
— Hugh Prather, author of *I Will Never Leave You*

"Reminds us that through the miracle of language we can embrace and share the wisdom of our hearts."
— Jerry Jampolsky, MD, author of *Love Is Letting Go of Fear*

"A wonderfully lucid and intelligent book, full of fascinating insights."
— Gabrielle Roth, author of *Maps to Ecstasy*

"Brings the magical world of existence into our everyday lives."
— Lynn Andrews, author of *Writing Spirit* and *Medicine Woman*

"Offers new perspectives on the process of rebirthing spiritual insight."
— Terence McKenna, author of *The Archaic Revival*

# write
## STARTS

## Other Books by the Author

*Write from the Heart:*
*Unleashing the Power of Your Creativity*

*Writing Spiritual Books:*
*A Bestselling Writer's Guide to Successful Publication*

*How to Write with a Collaborator,*
with Michael Larsen

*Follow Your Bliss: Discovering Your Inner Calling*
*and Right Livelihood*, with Susan J. Sparrow

*The Lens of Perception:*
*A User's Guide to Higher Consciousness*

*Spirit Animals and the Wheel of Life*

*Backland Graces: Four Novellas*

*Spirit Circle:*
*A Novel of Adventure and Shamanic Revelation*

*Zuni Fetishes:*
*Using Native American Objects for*
*Meditation, Reflection, and Insight*

*The Holotropic Mind*, with Stanislav Grof, MD

*Inner Guides, Visions and Dreams*

*Mind Jogger: A Problem Solving Companion*

# write
## STARTS

Prompts,
Quotes, and
Exercises to
Jumpstart Your
Creativity

# Hal Zina Bennett

New World Library
Novato, California

 New World Library
14 Pamaron Way
Novato, California 94949

Text design by Tracy Cunningham

Library of Congress Cataloging-in-Publication Data

Bennett, Hal Zina.
Write starts : prompts, quotes, and exercises to jumpstart your creativity /
    Hal Zina Bennett.
        p.    cm.
Includes bibliographical references.
ISBN 978-1-57731-689-3 (pbk. : alk. paper)
1.  Authorship—Problems, exercises, etc.  I. Title.
PN147.B465 2010
808'.042076—dc22                                    2009045905

First printing, February 2010
ISBN 978-1-57731-689-3
Printed in the United States on 30% postconsumer-waste recycled paper

g New World Library is a proud member of the Green Press Initiative.

10  9  8  7  6  5  4  3  2  1

*To the muse who lives in each of us,*
*still and quiet, awaiting our call . . .*

# Contents

# HOW TO USE THIS BOOK

*Amazing how many hours slip by while
planning how to use your time!*

— ANONYMOUS

I've been a working writer for more than thirty years, so when I sit down at my computer each morning, I pretty much know how I'm going to spend the day. There are good days and bad, of course, days when everything goes smoothly, even blissfully, and days when I am sure that my creative inspiration has abandoned me for a more worthy partner. But all in all, I usually have the time to wait it out — go for a walk, wash the dishes, rearrange bookshelves, walk out to the mailbox, clear the spam from my computer, strum my guitar (if nobody's within earshot), or email one of my writer friends to commiserate. I know that in time my brain will start functioning again, though it may take a couple of days. And if I have the presence of mind to remember, this feeling of being temporarily stalled isn't something new. It's happened thousands of times before. When I can be philosophical about it, I tell myself that it's part of a natural rhythm, creative gestation, a lull, a period for recharging my batteries. Well, to be honest, it can still be an uncomfortable experience. But I don't panic about it as much as I once did, mostly because I've been through it enough times to know that this creativity drought will not last and eventually my inspiration will return. However, it wasn't always like that.

For many years, before I started making a living in publishing, I worked at whatever paid the bills and whatever I was halfway good at doing — woodworker, handyman, land surveyor, set construction for a large theater company, chauffeur, tour bus driver, and teacher. I even worked as a cemetery groundskeeper one summer, digging graves, setting headstones, cutting grass, and planting flowers. In theory, my available time for writing was between 8 PM and midnight. But there were always other things to do during those hours: family responsibilities, recreation, watching TV, phone calls to friends and loved ones, taking a bath, puttering in the garden, reading, doing preparation for my day job, or working on the family car. (I've always owned "special needs" cars, meaning ones with more than 150,000 miles on the odometer, requiring an onboard mechanic — me.) So, my writing time probably averaged four or five hours a week.

When I was finally sitting down at my desk, ready to use those precious few hours I had for writing, the one thing that drove me half-crazy was discovering I had nothing to say. I'd clear the space for it. I'd tidy up my desk and shut off the phone. I had a fresh stack of paper in the printer, and I was pretty clear about which project

I wanted to work on. I placed my fingers on the keyboard and . . . nothing! My brain simply balked at the prospect of doing anything resembling work, and writing is definitely work. Good work, but work nevertheless. Knowing I had only limited time to write, getting my brain to work became increasingly crucial. Angst mounted as the minutes ticked by. I always compared such moments to rushing out to my car in the morning, a few minutes behind schedule, turning the key, and hearing that awful *urrrr urrah urrr* instead of the engine humming into action.

## Gimme Action!

This book was inspired by those exasperating moments of staring into a blank computer screen when I had limited time and energy to write. I know there are thousands of writers with scarce time for their art who face similarly maddening moments time and time again. I wanted to write the book that I'd always wished I had, something to get me through these frustrating periods. I envisioned a book with short readings — mostly between one and five pages — nothing ponderous that would eat up more of my precious time. I wanted readings that would jumpstart my brain so that I could make better use of whatever time I had before falling asleep or giving up in despair. Sort of like road service for stalled writers, the book could help me focus my attention, rev my engine, and get me on my way.

The book I imagined wasn't necessarily one that you'd pick up and read from cover to cover. When your time is limited and you're desperately trying to get your creativity flowing, you don't want to stop and read a whole book. You want to read a line or two, or maybe a few pages, ones that will give you inspiration or rattle your muse's cage or just get you focused so that you can do what you're sitting in front of the computer to do. So, *Write Starts* is that kind of book, one that you pick up, thumb through, and from which maybe randomly choose a single reading or quote that will turn out to be just the thing you need to activate your neurons. My recommendation is that you peruse this book so that you get some idea of what's in it. To help with that, I've written a short descriptive sentence for each reading listed in the table of contents.

If you are feeling stumped about a specific part of your craft, say character development, you might flip through the table of contents and find something to help you with that, say the "Checklist for Creating Characters" or the short reading titled "Where Characters Are Born."

You'll also find a few, I hope, amusing pieces, such as "Columbo's Notebook," on the subtler and seldom considered pros and cons of choosing a writer's notebook to carry around with you. There's a section on facing the sheer drudgery of writing, and another on the self-judgment that sometimes goes along with being a writer. And don't miss the piece called "Don't Be Scared of Virginia Woolf."

I've included short but insightful quotes by other authors, such as Isak Dinesen, May Sarton, Joan Didion, and Ernest Hemingway, writings to remind you that you are not alone in your struggles as a writer.

There are writing prompts, such as "The Old Bookstore," "Caught in the Act," and "Lonely Road," that offer vignettes around which you can tailor a short story or even a novel. But wouldn't that be stealing, you might ask? Not really. If you study the world's great literature closely, you'll find that there are story structures that authors use again and again. And as William Faulkner once said, "If a writer has to rob his mother, he will not hesitate; the 'Ode on a Graecian Urn' is worth any number of old ladies." Think of it this way: by the time you've added about sixty thousand of your own words to whatever story idea you've stolen, you will have more than made it your own. That's what storytellers do. As I am always reminding my students and clients, "There's nothing new under the sun — except you. And your unique voice will allow others to hear for the first time what others may have said a million times before."

## Your Writing Companion

There's a genre of books called "companions," with titles such as *The New Nursing Mother's Companion*, or *The Poet's Companion: A Guide to the Pleasures of Writing Poetry* (an actual book), or *A Traveler's Companion to Overnight Accommodations in Dublin*, or *The Beginning Chess Player's Companion*, or *A Stargazer's Companion*, or *The Ardent Moviegoer's Companion*. *Write Starts* is intended to have that sort of feeling about it; it's a companion for creative writers with limited time and unlimited enthusiasm for their favorite occupation. My view of companion books is that they should encourage interaction with their readers. That's the kind of book this one is. As such you should feel free to dog-ear pages and underline passages that have had special meaning for you, and certainly feel free to write in the margins. I've asked that my publisher provide a little extra white space — called "Field Notes" — at the end of the book for that purpose. In polite company, I know, writing in books is frowned upon, even considered vandalism. For others, it's a form of veneration, with each reader's marginal scrawlings becoming part of an ongoing conversation with the author. I'm obviously an advocate and member of this second camp.

If you're in the habit of reading books cover to cover, that's okay, too. Just make sure when you sit down to write, especially when time is of the essence, that this book is close at hand. Whenever you feel the need for inspiration, or when you need to be reminded of why you write, or maybe when you just need a quick summary of some aspect of your craft, pick this book up, thumb through it, and see what pops out at you. Often, a quick read is all you need; then you'll be back at the keyboard with your enthusiasm refreshed.

A few readings are longer and more detailed, in fact requiring a bit of time to explore. One such reading is "Magical Thinking: It's in the Cards," which describes a powerful creative tool that uses Tarot cards — a standard divination deck available in many bookstores. I tell in that reading how to use the cards to jog your creative mind and sense of discovery for developing a chapter outline, for organizing your book, for developing rich characters, or for working out dynamics between characters in a story you're writing. Use the same system for developing ideas, or for organizing a nonfiction work. This process may seem complicated at first, maybe even off the wall, but play with it on your own and you'll find that it really works.

If there are areas of study that you want to delve into more deeply, explore the annotated bibliography I've provided, in which I tell about some of my favorite writing books. For each book there's a paragraph describing what I thought was that author's most important contribution. These are not book reviews, just my own effort to share with my readers what I found valuable in each of the books.

## Make It Your Own

There are a couple of books on my shelves that are held together with rubber bands because the glued bindings have long since given way. These books are thickened at the corners with all the pages I've dog-eared. Long passages are underlined and special notations are written on the blank back sides of the covers. Like the worn fur and patched holes of a child's favorite stuffed toy or *blankie*, the wrinkled pages, marginal scrawls, and broken bindings testify not to the reader's abuse or disrespect but to his admiration and gratitude. I would only hope that this modest book of mine might suffer such fate at its readers' hands.

Make this book your own, and use it as you will. Randomly open it to the nearest reading or quote when you're feeling stuck, or use the table of contents to return to a favorite reading or one that seems like it might be helpful for a particular challenge you're facing right now. And if there's a favorite quote that you don't find here and you want to remember, copy it down in the "field notes" section.

Put yourself in these pages whenever you can — it's all part of awakening the best in yourself.  ·

# write
## STARTS

# GET UNREAL

Legend has it that Picasso once got into a discussion with a neighbor who looked at his paintings and told the artist that while his colors were nice and the picture was very pleasant, he should try making them a bit more realistic. Otherwise, he advised, nobody would know what Picasso's paintings were supposed to be about. The artist, exercising a rare amount of patience, nodded thoughtfully and asked his neighbor if he had an example of what he meant by *realistic*.

"Ah, yes, I do!" The neighbor quickly reached into his pocket, brought out his wallet, and handed over a photo of his wife for Picasso to see. "Now that's what I call realistic," he proclaimed.

Picasso took the photo in his hand, turned it this way and that, studied it from every angle, then handed it back to its owner. "She's awfully small and flat," he said.

In writing as with painting, there's an ongoing dialogue about what's real. Is the author's description of the house realistic? Is the communication between characters true to life? Is the story credible — could it happen in real life? Is the motivation of a character psychologically plausible? Is this or that action physically possible?

Sooner or later writers come to the full realization that

the reality depicted on the page or on the canvas of the painter has its own reality and is not a copy of life. The ultimate question we need to ask ourselves is, *Does it work as a story and on its own terms?*

Consider Franz Kafka's short story *The Metamorphosis*, about a man who turns into a bug. It couldn't happen in real life but within the framework of the story it is convincing. Nor does that author try to convince us that it's possible for humans to turn into bugs. However, he creates a reality on the page that causes us to identify with the poor victim, so much so that our skin crawls. We suffer with Kafka's character, with his bewilderment, and then with his abject horror at what's happening to him.

How does Kafka draw us into this reality? As readers we must, of course, be willing to go along with what the author creates. It's that *willing suspension of disbelief* thing all over again. In this particular story, Kafka accomplishes this with the first sentence: "As Gregor Samsa awoke one morning from uneasy dreams he found himself transformed in his bed into a gigantic insect." The author never attempts to explain how this happened or to justify its feasibility. Instead, he focuses our attention on what Gregor is experiencing. He describes, well, nothing more or less than what any normal person would experience if he woke up one morning to find he had become a giant insect!

At first Gregor's reactions are very human: he notes the size and number of his insect legs, then a framed photo on his wall, then the alarm clock that reminds him, with horror, that he's late for work. Many of his responses are downright mundane, which oddly enough makes us believe the story even more. For example, he looks out the window and sees that the sky is overcast and it "made him quite melancholy." He also struggles to make the horrible reality of his metamorphosis go away, "shutting his eyes to keep from seeing his struggling legs."

As time goes on and Gregor becomes increasingly bug-like, he discovers that his feet have a kind of stickiness that gives him traction with the floor, that his efforts to speak only produce strange, undecipherable sounds, and that his appearance horrifies his parents and his beloved sister. Through trial and error, and her own loving kindness, his sister discovers that in his present manifestation as a bug he likes rotting foods and notes that he seems repelled by fresher foods. In fact, he drags the decomposing food away from the fresh so that he can better savor his consumption of them.

The ludicrousness of this story is made believable through the author's ability to describe the very human reactions of his protagonist. While we might not believe it possible for *Homo sapiens* to turn into bugs, we can imagine the experience of being rendered helpless, imprisoned by our own bodies, and alienated from our loved ones. In the end, that's the message we go away with, made possible by creating a reality that could exist only in fiction but that is nevertheless meaningful and purposeful, reminding us of the limits of our own mortality.

Using literary devices such as Kafka does in *Metamorphosis*, write a few paragraphs, or even a short story, about what it might be like to wake up one morning to find that you are living in a world and perhaps a body very different from your own. Create a reality that could exist only on paper, yet that is credible in whatever terms you set up. This could be anything from being an animal in the wild to being an inanimate object. Maybe it's a reality existing on a different planet, or in a parallel universe, or in an imagined world that nobody has ever heard of. The experience of the characters you create could be horrifying or wonderful, pleasing and filled with discovery and insight, or as limiting and dreadful as turning into a bug. But the bottom line is that this is a reality completely of your own making — and certainly not "small and flat" like the photo of Picasso's neighbor.

*The process of writing, any form of creativity,*
*is a power intensifying life.*

## — RITA MAE BROWN
*STARTING FROM SCRATCH*

# CONTRADICTION AND PARADOX

Many students of human nature say that recognizing and coming to terms with contradiction and paradox is one of the key challenges of life; how can something be both true and false, both pleasurable and painful, both expanding and limiting? For example, in caring deeply about anything, we open doors not only for the pleasure of our own passions for a person, activity, place, idea, or thing but for the possibility of loss, disappointment, hurtful misunderstandings, and even betrayal. Similarly, making a choice to commit to one path in life means that we must give up other possibilities along the way. You might also consider that having knowledge or wisdom may provide its own satisfaction and expansiveness yet carry the greater burden and responsibility of awareness and pain.

Contradiction and paradox apply in nearly every area of our lives, be it with relationships, finances, education, developing a skill, ownership (of anything), having a passion for beautiful things, having a personal or spiritual practice, or holding a serious goal to have or achieve almost anything. George Santayana, twentieth-century philosopher, poet, and literary and cultural critic, said, "The world is a perpetual caricature of itself; at every moment it is the mockery and the contradiction of what it is pretending to be."

Think of a contradiction or memorable paradox in your own life. This could apply in the case of any choice or experience where there could be, or already was, a simultaneous plus and minus, pro and con, pleasure and pain, expansion and contraction, or gain and loss. The contradiction or paradox may have been a *potential* that made the decision difficult or a reality that you had to live with after making the decision. Write this as fiction or nonfiction, poetry or even song.

# TREASURE GARDEN

While she's working in her garden Samantha (you can call her anything you like) strikes a hard metal object with her trowel. She proceeds to dig around this obstacle, wanting to remove whatever it is to make room for her plants. But she soon discovers what it is that her trowel has struck. It appears to be the lid of an ancient metal chest. She digs around it with considerable care and finally lifts it out. It is much heavier than she would have judged it to be by its size.

Once the chest is out of the hole she begins inspecting it more closely. There is a huge bronze padlock on it. She remembers that when she bought this house, some years before, she'd found a beautifully crafted skeleton key hanging from a hook in a closet. It was so unusual that she kept it, displaying it among her collection of curios on a shelf in her living room. She runs inside, grabs the key, then returns to the chest. After blowing the dirt out of the keyhole, she carefully inserts the key, and the lock opens! She pries open the lid, whose hinges groan because they are rusty and corroded.

The chest open, she finds a large parchment envelope inside, stained and yellowed with age. With utmost care she lifts it out and sets it aside. There is something more in the chest. She now sees what appears to be a brittle and moldering leather packet, secured by two leather straps with silver buckles.

She turns her attention back to the parchment envelope and carefully opens it. Inside is a handwritten letter, also on parchment, which is amazingly well preserved. The writing is executed in a flowery script that she can barely read. It describes the contents of the leather packet, which she has not yet unwrapped, and tells why the box was buried.

Now it's your turn to take over the story. In your own words, tell what the note reveals. Describe Samantha's feelings as she lifts the leather packet from the old chest, unbuckles the straps, and peels back the brittle leather to reveal the contents. You, of course, will decide what she finds and what happens after that. Take the story as far as you wish to take it. Maybe you can even turn it into a novel!

*The puzzle that I'm now trying to unravel is
suggested by the observation that the creative
person, in the inspirational phase of the creative furor,
loses his past and his future and lives only
in the moment. He is all there, totally immersed,
fascinated and absorbed in the present, in the
current situation, in the here-now, with
the matter-in-hand.*

— **ABRAHAM H. MASLOW**
*THE FARTHER REACHES OF HUMAN NATURE*

# YOU DO IT SO WELL

We are often blind to the things we ourselves are best at doing in life. It is not that we're overly modest or that we have a self-esteem issue or that we don't want to draw attention to ourselves by owning our accomplishments or skills; it's more a matter of taking what we do for granted. It's just something we do. Maybe it's so easy for us that we can't imagine it being a big deal for anyone else. We might not notice that others can't do it or that they don't do it as effortlessly or as well as we do it.

This is not to say that there aren't more dysfunctional reasons for being blind to what we do best. I recall a man in a seminar I was teaching who I happened to know was an excellent pastry chef. When he was asked to write about something he was exceptionally good at, he made no mention of his bakery skills. During the break I asked him why he didn't mention this. "Oh, that's just what I do for a living," he replied. "I come from a family of chefs. It's something I can do in my sleep."

I argued that, regardless of how easy it was for him, he was exceptional at what he did, so would he please try to write about it. He finally did write something. But what came out was that he felt like a failure because his father and his older sister were both top-rated and well-paid chefs in five-star restaurants. Meanwhile, he struggled financially as a baker at a co-op coffee shop and bakery. Any time he saw his father or sister, they invariably got into a discussion of how talented he was and how he was wasting his talent working for little money for a low-prestige organization. He wrote how he looked upon his talent as a burden rather than a gift.

Once he'd described these things in writing, he got in touch with the fact that he really did take a great deal of pride in his skills — and loved baking. He went on to write a piece about his skills, describing in considerable detail the experience of baking and the pleasure he got from others enjoying his creations.

The lesson for us here is if we find ourselves confronting negative feelings around what we do best, we may first need to write about that experience. Like the baker, we may find our way clear to write about our gifts.

*Every time I start on a new book, I am a beginner again. I doubt myself, I grow discouraged, all the work accomplished in the past is as though it never was, my first drafts are so shapeless that it seems impossible to go on with the attempt at all, right up until the moment…when it has become impossible not to finish it.*

— **SIMONE DE BEAUVOIR**
*FORCE OF CIRCUMSTANCE*

# NATURALLY SUPERNATURAL

You've been invited to visit a friend who recently moved into an old fixer-upper in a small town in the Midwest. The town is quaint and picturesque, with a population of around five thousand. The house is huge, a two-story Victorian in great disrepair. Your friend tells you that previous renters had complained the house was haunted and friends informed her that there is a legend about the place that goes back in history about 150 years. However, your friend, who has restored several old houses, shrugs off the idea, saying it is pure superstition and to pay no attention to the rumors circulating about the place. She loves the old house and doesn't want to hear anything bad about it, so she has refused to listen to any of the stories people tell. Old houses, she argues, make funny noises, usually due to structural problems. The ghosts have a way of disappearing after a new foundation is poured and rotting walls are repaired and squeaky hinges are replaced.

That night you are shown to a large, nicely furnished room on the second floor. Stepping into it is like stepping into the past. You quickly fall asleep. Then, around 3 AM you are awakened by a strange sound and are alarmed to realize that someone is in your room. You hear a woman's voice calling your name, and a hand on your shoulder gently shakes you. You bolt upright even as the woman tries to assure you that she means no harm and is not a ghost. Rather, she is seeking your help. You turn on the bedside light. It's a real woman — and, no, this is not a dream. The woman pulls up a chair, sits down, and begins to tell you her story. For several years she has been living, along with one other person, in secret rooms hidden in the basement passages of the house. More than a hundred years ago her great-grandfather built this place, and nobody outside her family knows of the underground rooms and passageways. Now the woman fears she must move and thus reveal a truth that will result in great danger to her, the second resident of the secret rooms, and the present owner of the house. She shares a secret that makes you part of a mystery that you cannot ignore.

Pick up this story at any point that you wish, telling it in your own words and going on to reveal the mystery.

*As well as being good company for writers, cats and dogs can make good muses. (If you love animals, you'll understand. If you don't, just skip this.) My cats, Stuart and Charlotte, have listened to more bad prose read aloud, to more moaning about how hard it is to write, as well as to bizarre moments of my over-the-top optimism — and they never lose their cool. They never say to me,* Oh, stop whining, and find some real work, *or* Don't count your chickens, cookie, *or* Don't you think this might be a little too personal to write about?

## — BARBARA ABERCROMBIE
*COURAGE AND CRAFT: WRITING YOUR LIFE INTO STORY*

# FIND YOUR INNER DOG...OR CAT

Write from the point of view of a dog, cat, or other animal. Think of the animal's inherent limitations and abilities — extraordinary abilities in particular — as you do. For example, writing from a dog's point of view you might focus attention on the canine's highly developed sense of smell. If I were a dog sniffing the cuff of my human's pant leg, I might know exactly where he's been — *across the street with that blond lady who lives with three cats and smells like roses and cooking cabbage.* At the same time, I might be quite puzzled about the funny noises humans make whenever they kneel down to pat my head and I lick their faces — *awrh poochy-poo suchawunner fulfelle izent tea yesseeeiz.*

Particularly look for ways to use irony, to have your animal narrator bring attention to human behavior or the idiosyncrasies of another species. In the example, the dog pokes a bit of fun at the blond lady across the street as well as human language. Similarly, as a cat you might be preoccupied with scents, similar to dogs in that respect, but maybe you would put yourself above dogs — literally and figuratively — because of your capacity to leap and climb. You could do this by talking about how much fun it is to get one of your canine counterparts to chase you across the yard and up a tree. Then you watch with a contented smile, resting on a sun-bleached branch as the silly dog creature runs around below, sniffing at the ground in search of your trail while it never occurs to him, not even once, to look up in the tree.

If you happen to be one of the more fortunate humans who has animal companions in your life, try looking at yourself from the point of view of that animal, including its feelings of loyalty and affection for you. Or maybe, contrariwise, there's an animal in your life whom you view as a nuisance or even an enemy: the deer who comes down at night and dines on your flowers, the bat that's taken up residence in the rafters of your garage, the gopher who decimates your garden every summer. Describe an incident that happened from the deer or the bat's or the gopher's point of view, not from your own place of frustration or anger.

Don't overlook creatures who might seem like the most unlikely candidates as authors: the spider who weaves intricate gossamer patterns in the trellis outside your kitchen window, the goldfish who turns and swims eagerly toward you whenever you approach its bowl, the blue jay who scolds you when you take out the garbage, the big catfish swimming in the pond in the park near your home, perhaps even a housefly.

Try using both a first-person and a third-person narrative voice in this exercise.

*First person of a cat: "I began plotting my next move as I lay on the fat branch of the apple tree, basking in the morning sun and watching the stupid dog nosing around in the dirt searching for my scent."*

*Third person: "K. T. McPheline lay contentedly on the fat branch of the apple tree, basking in the morning sun, grinning as the dog ran around the backyard with his nose to the ground, with no idea where that troublesome cat had gone."*

Maybe you'd like to really push the envelope and play for comic relief, as in the story titled *Fup*, by Jim Dodge. Fup, as the story goes, is a female mallard duck. In one scene we find her perched on the seat back of a pickup truck in a drive-in movie theater, with Granddaddy and Tiny, his human companions:

*Fup's favorite movies were romances, whether light and witty or murderously tragic. She watched intently from her roost on the back of the seat, occasionally tilting her head to quack in sympathy at the problems assailing love. She would not tolerate Granddaddy's derisive and consistently obscene comments, and after she'd almost torn off his ears a few times he settled for quiet mumbling. Tiny watched without comment.*

I like doing this writing exercise from time to time, mainly to expand my capacity for taking another person's point of view. We naturally project ourselves into whatever characters we create, human or other-than-human.

But the animal exercise forces us to think about characteristics that are normally quite foreign to us — the dog's finely tuned sense of smell, for instance, or the cat's capacity for scrambling up a tree. Translating that lesson to human terms, you might take on characteristics that are quite outside your first-hand experience, such as writing from their point of view or taking on the mythological attributes of a vampire or centaur.

Each time I do this writing practice I think of Dylan Thomas's *Portrait of the Artist as a Young Dog.* He didn't actually assume the character of a dog in that collection of stories but maybe had he lived past his thirty-ninth birthday he would have thought of that, too. I think if I were to write a memoir of my life that way I'd assume the character of a cat. Hmm. *Portrait of the Author as a Young Cat.*

*I know some very great writers, writers you love who write beautifully and have made a great deal of money, and not one of them sits down routinely feeling wildly enthusiastic and confident. Not one of them writes elegant first drafts. All right, one of them does, but we do not like her very much. We do not think she has a rich inner life or that God likes her or can even stand her.*

— **ANNE LAMOTT**
*BIRD BY BIRD*

# WHERE DREAMS COME TRUE

Late one night the phone rings, awakening you from a vivid, exciting, and (perhaps) disturbing dream that involves a friend of yours. You pick up the phone and are surprised to hear the voice of the person you were just dreaming about. The caller tells you about something that is presently happening in her (or his) life and asks, rather desperately, to come over and talk with you. This person knows how late it is but assures you this is urgent. Even from the little you know so far, you realize that your friend is describing exactly the situation that you were dreaming. It is as if your dream life and real life have seamlessly joined.

At first you are reluctant to tell your friend about your dream, but because of the urgency of her situation, you invite her to come over and talk. Perhaps she can sleep on your couch or in an extra room.

Tell what happens when you get together. Explain how it could be that there is this seamless connection between your dream and your friend's situation in the real world. Does the dream reveal something that has still not been revealed in real life? Does the dream offer a real-life solution or a way of avoiding inevitable disaster? Are there any conflicts or double binds involved if you and your friend accept the dream as an accurate prophecy? Could following it in this way worsen the problem? Take the story as far as you wish.

# A MARK IN TIME

You are meeting a woman friend for coffee, or perhaps a drink, at a place familiar to both of you. It's a pleasant enough spot, genteel and with a usually polite clientele. You arrive a half-hour early, expecting that you'll have to wait for your friend. There are fewer than a dozen people in the place. You sit down at a small table where you can watch the door and where you are sure your acquaintance will see you when she eventually turns up.

Toward the shadowy back of the room, you see three people sitting in one of the booths — two men and a woman. The woman is turned slightly away from you so that you see only her back and her long hair, which you recognize because of the idiosyncratic way she fixes it. The three people in the booth are engaged in a heated argument that is becoming louder and more heated by the second. You watch out of the corner of your eye, curious but anxious about the angry tones of the trio's voices.

The woman briefly turns toward the room, her face confirming that this is your friend, erasing any doubts you may have had about her identity. You raise your hand in greeting but she fixes you with a stony glare, telegraphing a warning for you to keep your distance.

The man sitting opposite her snaps his head in your direction, having noticed the exchange between you and the woman. Suddenly all is quiet at the booth. The squabbling stops. The man stares at you for a moment, gets to his feet, and starts across the room toward your table. And now you recognize his face. He is someone from your distant past — and you freeze at the sight of him.

In your own words, describe what happens next. Using dialogue and narrative, reveal to the reader:

1. The identity of the man and how you know him

2. The identity of the woman

3. The identity of the second man

4. What the quarrel at the booth was about

5. Where the story goes from there.

# CHILDHOOD REMEMBRANCE

In her autobiography, mystery writer Agatha Christie wrote that "one of the luckiest things that can happen to you in life...is to have a happy childhood." Given the intrinsic hazards of growing up, one wonders how many of us could claim such good fortune. Still, childhood is a rich source of material for every writer.

One of the chief hazards that childhood development experts describe is that we start out in life with an overabundance of curiosity and a dearth of experience. Our bountiful curiosity can draw us into circumstances that we haven't the experience to comprehend or consider the consequences of, sometimes leading to painful misunderstandings, emotional wounds, or physical danger.

A psychologist friend of mine tells how, at five or six, fueled by his fascination with Superman stories, he suited up in the Halloween costume of his superhero and leapt from the second-story window of his bedroom. Instead of flying, as he fully expected to do, he ended up in the hospital with a broken collarbone and arm, spared from worse injuries by the branches of the flowering plum that broke his fall. His bones and bruises healed perfectly but the painful experience is still vivid in his memory. Today he tells this story to his patients to illustrate the fact that there's a difference between the world we create in our minds and the world *out there*. While most of us, even as small children, know the consequences of leaping from high places, we have all suffered the wounds of discovering that there's a difference between the world we hold in our minds and the world out there.

As a writing exploration, recall an early time in your childhood when you encountered this fact. The range of experience is vast, from a great disappointment you felt when something you'd dearly looked forward to was canceled at the last moment to the serious betrayal of an adult you had trusted and loved. As you write about this experience, do so not from your adult perspective looking back in time but from the child's perspective in the time the event occurred.

To do this, take the following into account:

- Your physical size in relation to objects in the physical world around you

- Your knowledge or innocence then about the ways of the world

- Feelings you had toward other people — children or adults

- How empowered or helpless you felt — both before and after the experience

- What you believed was happening and what really was happening

After you've finished writing about this experience from the child's point of view, write a paragraph or so from your present adult perspective. Tell how you are still affected by this experience and what, if any, lessons you learned from it that are valuable to you today.

*I learned that you should feel when writing, not like Lord Byron on a mountain top, but like a child stringing beads in kindergarten — happy, absorbed and quietly putting one bead on after another.*

— **BRENDA UELAND**
*IF YOU WANT TO WRITE*

# CHANGE OF MIND

Write about a person or event that changed the way you experience or think about your life, taking the time to craft this writing — fiction or nonfiction — using physical description, dialogue, or any other storytelling skills you wish. This could be something that happened between you and another person — adult or child — in your life.

The experience you describe might be a dreadful event, such as a natural disaster, a war experience, or another life-threatening incident. It could be about the birth or death of someone you love. Or it could be a seemingly minor, *everyday* happening — your child's first steps, being awestruck by photos of planet Earth from the moon, an out-of-the-blue reconciliation with someone from whom you'd been alienated, the remarkable scent of a wildflower. Even the most commonplace moments can sometimes contain the essence of personal foment that forever alter how you see the world.

Most of us have been deeply affected by a social or historical event that touched not only our own lives but the lives of many others. This might be anything from the assassination of a world leader, such as John F. Kennedy or Martin Luther King Jr., to the terrorist attack of the

Twin Towers in New York City in 2001. Similarly, there are social calamities such as the Great Depression of the 1930s or our more recent mortgage crisis that threatens the homes of millions of people. There are also happier events such as the Woodstock Festival of 1969, about which books are still being written. If the events that changed your mind were like these, consider doing a little research and bringing in concrete facts about that time in history; establish tie-ins between your own inner life and conditions that thousands or even millions of other people are aware of.

As you write, focus your attention on the "before and after" components of the experience. What was it that released you from social, cultural, religious, spiritual, or psychological blinders that once narrowed your worldview? What did you learn that got you involved in an activity, vocation, or relationship that you feel might otherwise never have been possible? What were you able to make a part of your personal experience that might have otherwise been impossible?

*Human relations just are not fixed in their orbits like the planets — they're more like galaxies, changing all the time, exploding into light for years, then dying away.*

**— MAY SARTON**
*CRUCIAL CONVERSATIONS*

# CAUGHT IN THE ACT

You are at a coffee shop enjoying a chai or a cappuccino after working out at the gym. You are the only customer in the shop, and you've just sat down at one of the small tables. Two people wearing black ski masks and carrying guns burst in. You watch, stunned, as one of the robbers guards the door while the other yells at the cashier to open the cash register and hand everything over. The cashier tells him that most of the cash was removed an hour before and put in a safe to which nobody in the store has a combination. The robber at the door screams, "Forget it. Let's get out of here," then disappears outside.

The second robber, now alone, rushes for the door. You suddenly feel heroic. You kick a chair into his path and he stumbles over it. Momentarily, his mask slips off and you recognize him as Nick, a coworker at the computer company where you work. You and he exchange horrified glances. He gathers his wits about him, says something to you in a spine-chilling tone, then leaps to his feet and in an instant is gone.

For a moment you sit there in a fog, wondering what to do. Nick has always been a decent guy and was always friendly toward you. In fact, a very close friend of yours has been dating him for months and there has been no indication whatsoever that he would ever commit a criminal act. Why would he have done what he did? Had he changed? Had he hidden this side of himself so successfully that nobody had seen it? The words he muttered to you just before running away echo in your mind.

Your first inclination is to talk to him, give him a chance to explain himself. After all, nobody was hurt and nothing was stolen. But now you notice that the person at the counter is on the phone, obviously quite agitated. You know the police will be here at any moment.

It's your turn to tell the rest of the story.

*Sometimes, when I find I haven't written a single sentence after scribbling whole pages, I collapse on my couch and lie there dazed, bogged in a swamp of despair, hating myself and blaming myself for this demented pride that makes me pout after a chimera. A quarter of an hour later, everything has changed; my heart is pounding with joy.*

— **GUSTAVE FLAUBERT**
IN A LETTER TO LOUISE COLET

# DON'T BE SCARED
# OF VIRGINIA WOOLF

One of a writer's most difficult challenges is facing the daily ups and downs of the work. Sometimes the writing goes well. Everything flows. You turn out a number of pages that you feel are good, and the process itself is fulfilling or even ecstatic. But there are other days when it's just the opposite; not only is the process frustrating, slow, and unproductive but the few sentences you do get down on paper are embarrassing, clumsy, and irrelevant.

In her book *A Life of One's Own: A Guide to Better Living Through the Work and Wisdom of Virginia Woolf*, Ilana Simons discusses how there were many days when Woolf produced fifty or fewer words. Woolf herself reports that sometimes what she turned out made her feel ashamed, either because the crafting itself was inept (she felt) or because it showed a side of her she would rather not reveal to strangers. It's alleged that she said she'd too frequently written passages that made her "cheeks burn."

I don't know any writers who haven't experienced such moments. The worst of it isn't that our cheeks burn but that what we've written discourages us from writing anything at all. On such days we're lucky if we get ten words down on paper. I'm not talking about everyday writer's block but rather our feelings about ourselves as writers, how we can leap to the conclusion that we have no talent, that we're sloppy writers, that the life experiences we draw upon are banal or silly, or that we don't know how to access our creative resources well enough to be a writer.

As masochistic as it might sound, it's been my observation that the creative consciousness includes this capacity for being abysmally self-critical and mean-spirited. Do we need psychotherapy or extensive self-analysis to rid ourselves of this inclination? What you learn in time, if you have the courage or tenacity to stick with it, is that these lows are part and parcel of the creative process. The highs take care of themselves; they motivate us to reach for them again and again. At the opposite pole, the lows can be painful, and we may expend a huge amount of energy resisting them or trying to escape their sting.

What Ilana Simons discovered in her study of Virginia Woolf's life was that the author got through the lows of the writing experience by keeping a work schedule and holding to it religiously. She wrote even though there were days when she only produced fifty words that made her cringe when she read them back to herself. The next day she still stuck to her schedule and wrote another fifty words, and so on. It is a lesson probably every successful writer learns — to work, in Woolf's words, *shamelessly but consistently*. Simons had it right when she said, "It's like closing your eyes to what's happening in the moment, trusting consistency itself," in this case, consistency of the routine.

As a working writer for more than thirty years, I've learned that there's a certain ratio of successful to less-than-successful writing. Thankfully, that ratio leans toward the successful more often than not. If you keep writing and you don't allow yourself to take your daily self-criticism too seriously, or at least not let it stop you, it'll all come to something good. Your daily work doesn't have to be exceptional. It doesn't even have to please you. As with nearly everything in life, you get better by showing up and *doing* it shamelessly and consistently.

*The characters who come to life on the page or on the stage are the ones that have passed through the storyteller's imagination. Your readers already "know" people as well as real people ever know each other. They turn to fiction in order to know people better than they can ever know them in real life.*

**— ORSON SCOTT CARD**
*CHARACTERS AND VIEWPOINT*

# THE FIVE SENSES

Whenever possible, use the five senses to enliven your writing. Do it whether you are writing fiction or nonfiction. The five senses can even be useful in writing a self-help book whenever you may want to spruce up an anecdote illustrating a point you're making or a process you're describing. Here are examples of how other writers have used the five senses. Each of the following focuses on one or two senses:

### Sight

*Among twenty snowy mountains,*
*the only moving thing*
*Was the eye of a blackbird.*

> — From "Thirteen Ways of Looking at a Blackbird,"
> by Wallace Stevens

### Sound

*Sling your knuckles on the bottoms of the happy tin pans, let*
*your trombones ooze, and go husha-husha-hush with the*
*slippery sand-paper.*

> — From "Jazz Fantasia," by Carl Sandburg

### Touch

*She went out from the rock, caught the surge around it and went downstream to a place where she grabbed maple branches and swung around on her belly to face the current. The water lifted her up and when she spread her legs let her down. She closed her eyes and let the water break around her nose and lifted, against her breasts, arched her back, the current against her hips, opened her legs and sank down. She imagined herself among salmon (against her, opened her legs and sank down), swimming gently among salmon, (lifting, sank down), until the light seemed brighter, birds quieter, and she was wide-eyed, afraid of being seen, that the privacy of her morning had been broken like an eggshell, and she came out on the bank.*

— From *River Notes: The Dance of Herons*,
by Barry Holstun Lopez

### Taste-Smell

*They sat cross-legged on the soft down quilt that Isha had spread out on the warm redwood deck. The sun was low in the sky now and the air was at last cooling. "You can smell the lavender," she said, inhaling deeply, as if having detected some hidden danger in the air. "It's spicy this year, almost like cedar." Her voice became hoarse, tentative.*

*He cut her a thin slice of warm ripe peach, one of three they'd bought at the roadside stand that morning, and placed it gingerly between her lips. She smiled, tipped back her head and let the fragrant morsel fall against her teeth. The sugary juices gushed exquisitely over her tongue as she tenderly pressed the soft damp flesh of the fruit against the roof of her mouth. Savoring the rich taste, she gazed out over the lush, green forest that separated them from the highway. The pungent scent of redwood curled in her nostrils, secretly reassuring.*

*Clearly, he did not yet suspect.*

— From an unpublished story by Hal Zina Bennett

*I was trying to write then and I found the
greatest difficulty, aside from knowing truly what
you really felt, rather than what you were supposed
to feel, and had been taught to feel, was to put down
what really happened in action; what the actual things
were which produced the emotion that you experienced
…the real thing, the sequence of motion and fact which
made the emotion and which would be as
valid in a year or in ten years or, with luck and if
you stated it purely enough, always.*

— **ERNEST HEMINGWAY**
*DEATH IN THE AFTERNOON*

# MAGICAL THINKING:
# IT'S IN THE CARDS

I'm a great believer in *random selection* as a creative tool. It's a term that comes from statistics and science, referring to individual selections made entirely by chance from a larger group or set. The selections made are truly random when each individual within the group has exactly the same probability of being selected.

What's so great about random selection? It gets you out of your own head, your own habits and routines. With the right tools, it's a way of tricking yourself into thinking *outside the box*, that is, coming up with ideas, images, qualities, and actions that are more innovative or varied than you might otherwise dream you had in you. Used properly, it's a great brainstorming tool, providing just the right amount of structure and openness to explore the unknown.

One of the most accessible random selection tools is the Tarot deck. It's a deck of cards designed for divinatory use. Each card is illustrated, often with symbolic meanings, with its own characteristics and values. The most popular Tarot decks are the *Rider-Waite Tarot Deck*; the

*Motherpeace Cards*; and the *Medicine Cards*. Another excellent system is *The Book of Runes*, based on the Viking Oracles, which instead of cards uses small tiles with simple symbols etched on them. These decks are intended as divinatory systems but, as you'll see, that's not how I use them here.

You can find these decks at most larger bookstores, online, or in shops specializing in spiritual books and supplies. Most come with a small book of instructions that describe the meaning of each card. There are also books that go into considerable detail about their interpretations. The way I use them for writers is, as far as I know, unique. There are three basic ways I use these systems:

1. Breaking through writer's blocks

2. Developing characters for stories

3. Organizing chapter outlines for books

*Note:* The following instructions will be most helpful to you if you have one of these divination systems in your hands.

## Breaking Through Writer's Blocks: Root-Gain-Solution

For the serious writer, writer's blocks can be very painful. No matter what you try, it seems you can't get a single sentence down on paper. To break through, or at least explore what internal issues may be causing the block, do the following:

*Step 1:* Form a question or request that you wish to have answered by the cards. It's important to form the question in a positive way. For example, "What do I need to know or do to free myself to write?" Not, "Why am I so screwed up that I can't write?"

*Step 2:* Shuffle the deck while holding your question in your mind.

*Step 3:* Fan out the cards, facedown, on the table before you.

*Step 4:* Randomly select three cards, without looking at their faces. Place them on the table before you in this simple configuration:

*Step 5:* Turn over the first card and read it, or simply study the card itself and see what it suggests to you. The first card will tell you something about the *root cause* of the problem, in this case what has happened that has caused you to feel blocked. For example, I have just drawn the Five of Swords. The standard *Rider-Waite* card

depicts a disdainful-looking man holding three swords, with three other swords lying at his feet and two dejected-looking figures retreating from him. The simplest reading for this card is *loss, destruction*, or *degradation*. I ask myself what exactly this means to me, given this position of the card as a root cause of the problem. What I come up with is that two days before I got a rejection slip from a publisher for a story I'd written. I certainly felt dejected when I received it, since I believed it was a well-written piece. Then it occurs to me that perhaps I am feeling, "What's the use?" The rejection has caused me to feel defeated.

*Step 6:* Read the second card, *Gain*. This card asks us to reflect on something that we're gaining by clinging to this feeling of defeat and rejection. The card I draw is the Four of Pentacles. It depicts a crowned young man with a gold pentacle over his head, one in his hand, and one under each foot. The divinatory meaning simplified has to do with clinging to treasures one already possesses. Reflecting on this, it feels to me that perhaps I am clinging to past successes instead of going forward to create something new. Has the rejection slip

I received two days before triggered this reaction? This feels true to me. The message is that I need to come to peace with the rejection slip I'd received and stop holding on to my past successes to soothe my wounded pride. I go on to read the third card.

*Step 7:* The third card, *Solution*, will perhaps guide me to a way out of my present dilemma. The card I've drawn is Wheel of Fortune. Ah, this is great. The simplest reading of the card is *success, luck*, and *abundance*. What I take this to mean is that what I'm working on right now — or would be, if I didn't have writer's block — has the potential of turning out well. All I have to do is get over my reaction to the rejection slip and stop clinging to my previous accomplishments.

I go for a short walk to think over what I've come up with in the reading. By the time I return, I'm feeling more creative and dive right into my writing.

Now, you may ask, how do I know if my insights are true? Are they accurate readings of the cards? I have no way of knowing that, nor do I care. Whatever my reading of the cards, it is always my interpretations of their meanings that I work with. The random selection process afforded by the cards gets me out of my own way of thinking — to whatever degree that may be humanly possible. At the very least, I think about the problem I'm facing in a new way. For a moment I jump out of the box and maybe, just maybe, escape the limitations of my own thinking.

## Developing Characters

The second way I use the Tarot cards is to flesh out a character I'm working on in a story. For this I use a slightly more complex layout of the cards. This one looks like this:

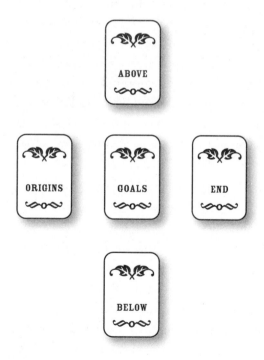

*Step 1:*   Shuffle the pack and draw five cards, always keeping them facedown, laying them out in the order shown. We're going to be looking at a villainous guy named Lomax with the purpose of making him a richer, more three-dimensional character.

*Step 2:*   The first card I select for Lomax is the *Origins* card, which turns out to be a Six of Pentacles. The simple reading for this is wealth and gifts. My interpretation is that my character comes from a privileged background, and that his parents were civic-minded and generous people.

*Step 3:*   The middle card is *Goals*. I draw the Ace of Wands here. This card seems to substantiate that Lomax's assets come from his family of origin — wealth passing from parents to son. He is inventive and entrepreneurial. He is beginning to look admirable, so far. Where exactly is this leading us? As the author I could decide this means that he embraces his creativity and makes good use of his inherited wealth. Or, I might decide that his inventiveness takes him in a very different direction, to cheat others in the family out of their inheritance. The card gets me thinking about all the ways that inventiveness might be used for either good or evil — or creating conflict between the two. In which direction will we go with our villain? Maybe the next card will provide a clue.

Step 4: I now draw the third card, the *End* card, forecasting how Lomax is going to end up. This is the Ten of Swords, a gruesome card, as it turns out. Pictured is a prone figure with ten swords piercing his body. The meaning of this card is clear: he ultimately ends up desolate and dead, maybe murdered? This is a fitting enough end for a villain.

Step 5: The fourth card is the one I call *Above*. It helps to define the higher purpose or ideals of the character, that is, what influences him or her from above. The card I draw is The World. This is ordinarily a very positive card, denoting assured success, a safe voyage, or change. Apparently, then, Lomax does pretty well for himself along the way.

Step 6: The fifth card, the *Below* card, is intended to help us define the lower, or darker, influences in the character's life. The one I draw here is the Four of Wands. This card is the very picture of success and the country life, the security and peace of prosperity and old, well-established wealth.

So what am I to make of all this? Is there a mistake? Everything appears to be so positive and bountiful for Lomax — except for his gruesome ending, pierced by the swords. But here I have the makings of an interesting villainous character. Of course! He comes from a privileged background. He enjoys a successful and even pastoral life, at least on the surface. But what hidden influences, what darkness or evil is at work in this man's life? Why and how does he misuse his gifts?

The cards have given me the foundation for a character who embraces many contradictory forces in his life. What we find in the cards presents the author with copious possibilities while still providing a framework for developing a villain who is perhaps all too human. He's innovative and wealthy and lives a life that most of us can only dream of. He begins life with every advantage the world offers — great parents, wealth, security, and apparently a creative and resolute mind. What does he do with his gifts, what fateful choices does he make that bring him to his violent end?

All of this was revealed through the layout and readings from the cards. And, if I ever need further help exploring his character, all I have to do is draw more cards and ask what each one tells me about my villain with his seemingly incongruous traits.

## Organizing Chapter Outlines

One of the more challenging tasks of writing a book is organizing it. That task is almost magically accomplished with the help of the cards. In dozens of workshops, and with hundreds of authors I've coached over the years, I've seen this process work over and over again, often to my own amazement. The first time was quite out of the blue. One of my students, Carla, was an intuitive counselor and very much at home working with Tarot cards. The class had been exploring character development and clearing writer's block, and at the end of one of our brainstorming sessions Carla mentioned that she was going half-crazy trying to organize her manuscript. Her book was about two-thirds written, but some of the chapters weren't quite coming together for her and she wasn't happy with the sequencing of the information. On a whim, I said let's try the cards.

We began by deciding, somewhat arbitrarily, how many chapters there would be. Carla said she wanted there to be eleven plus an introduction. She shuffled her Tarot cards, fanned them out facedown on the work table, and then picked out eleven chapter cards, plus one for the introduction. She now had a row of twelve cards, still facedown on the table before her. One by one, as the class watched, she began turning the cards over, starting with chapter 1. She first looked at each card and recited its meaning. Then she free-associated, naming how the material in the book related to each reading. She went through all eleven cards while one of her classmates recorded the session on her digital recorder. Amazingly, by the end not only did Carla have a plan for organizing the book, but she knew how she was going to reorganize three of the chapters and now knew what she needed to say in two of the chapters she hadn't even begun to write.

It takes a while to get used to this way of working. When we're stuck or we feel just plain wrung out and without a grain of creativity left, our brains long for order. We want a clear path to follow. But working with divination systems as I've described calls upon the right hemisphere of our brains, the ancient creative-intuitive capacities. Think of the Tarot deck as a bridge between the two hemispheres of your brain, assisting you in the passage from the linear to the intuitive. Above all, be playful with the process. Don't try to force anything; it will lead you where you didn't know you wanted to go, but you will be delighted when you arrive.

# CHEMISTRY OF CHARACTER INTERACTION

The *chemistry* between characters is a quality of relationship that often comes through between the lines of description or dialogue. The writer creates this chemistry in subtle ways, sometimes through dialogue, sometimes through physical description, and sometimes through the portrayal of the characters' inner thoughts and feelings. In the following two sentences from John Steinbeck's short story "Johnny Bear," we see all three of these techniques at work. The author introduces two characters simultaneously by describing one through the eyes of the other, even as his writing generates a certain chemistry between the characters. Note how Steinbeck's narrator-protagonist describes Fat Carl, the bartender and owner of the Buffalo Bar:

> *His face was sour, his tone downright unfriendly, and yet — I don't know how he did it. I know I felt gratified and warm when Fat Carl knew me well enough to turn his sour pig face to me and say with some impatience, "Well, what's it going to be?"*

Fat Carl is certainly unattractive ("face was sour"); intimidating ("his tone downright unfriendly"); edgy ("with some impatience"); and *swinish* ("his sour pig face"). He's probably not the kind of guy you or I would seek out as a friend. So what's behind the narrator's feelings of being "gratified and warm" as Fat Carl gets to know him? Therein lies the nucleus around which the chemistry of these two characters evolves.

As the story progresses, we learn that the narrator is new in town, a stranger in a strange place, without friends or acquaintances. The point at which he feels that Fat Carl "knew me well enough" signals the beginning of his feeling accepted into the Buffalo Bar community ("I felt gratified and warm"). He's no longer a stranger, and he feels good about that.

What makes the chemistry between these two characters work? Could it be that they have something in common, perhaps their secret loneliness, experienced by the narrator because he's a stranger in town and by the bartender because he's physically and personally off-putting to others? Beneath the surface, both characters are outsiders, and in that spark of familiarity they both find some comfort.

Try writing a paragraph or more revealing the chemistry between two people, using techniques like those Steinbeck employs in the previous excerpt: dialogue, physical description, and the portrayal of your characters' inner thoughts and feelings. This can involve fictional characters that you create, or it can be about a relationship in your own life.

Remember that the chemistry should come across *between the lines*. Note that Steinbeck never directly tells us that both of his characters in the example are lonely, or that they feel alienated, or that they otherwise feel distanced from other people. Yet this sense of personal isolation and disconnection comes through. The chemistry you reveal need not be this sense of separateness, of course. It can be love, longing, familiarity, regret, fear, dread, outright hostility, or any number of other emotions or states of mind.

# OUT ON A LIMB

Choose something you've always wanted to do but for some reason have not yet done. It might be that you've wanted to visit another country but have put it off because it was too expensive or you didn't have the time. Maybe you always wanted to parachute from an airplane or fly in a sail plane. Or you've dreamed of swimming with dolphins or snorkeling to watch beautiful fish in the tropics. Don't forget to consider things you may have wanted to do but were afraid you didn't have the skills or courage to do, such as performing as a stand-up comic before a large group of strangers or running for a political office or skiing a special mountain.

You may wish to start with a short paragraph about why you have always wanted to do whatever it is you've chosen to write about. Then tell how, because of a stroke of luck in your life, the opportunity to do it magically arose, giving you the green light. If money was what was holding you back, tell how that problem was solved. If your fears were holding you back, tell how you got up the courage to take this step. If lack of self-confidence was the hurdle you had to leap, describe why and how you were able to develop the skills you required to feel confident.

Remember, this is a creative process, so you can make up anything you wish. Be as fanciful or down-to-earth and realistic as you wish.

Finally, go on to describe yourself in the act of doing whatever it is you have wished to do. Portray as full and rich a picture of the experience as you can, including descriptions of your thoughts and emotions as well as what you see, hear, taste, touch, and smell.

*The creation of something new is not accomplished by the intellect but by the play instinct acting from inner necessity. The creative mind plays with the objects it loves.*

**— C. G. JUNG**
*PSYCHOLOGICAL TYPES*

# EMBERS OF PAST WOUNDS

All great writers revisit wounds of their pasts, for it is in doing so that they find the greatest drama, the most affecting stories, the conflict and potential character development for their work. It is also here that we uncover life-changing revelations. Revisiting such events of our own requires that we muster up the courage to look at even the most unpleasant or painful or embarrassing parts of our lives. When we do this, our creative fires are fueled, without which a writer is little more than a typist with an attitude.

Abigail Adams, in a letter to her son John Quincy Adams, said, "It is not in the still calm of life, or the repose of a pacific station, that great characters are formed .... The habits of a vigorous mind are formed in contending with difficulties." Still, it is human nature to avoid such hot spots in our lives; withdrawing from pain and discomfort is, after all, instinctual. That's what keeps us from putting ourselves in harm's way.

Recall one or more challenging events from your life and think of ways you might use them in your writings. For example, in a self-help book or article you might use an anecdote about overcoming your shyness to inspire readers to develop greater assertiveness. In fiction, you might use your memories of being harassed by the school bully to create a villainous character and his victim's terrified response. Think how these experiences might be written to describe turning points, or overcoming great adversity, or forgiving someone who hurt you deeply, or discovering something you'd rather not admit about yourself.

# SYMPATHIES FOR THE VILLAIN

Creative writing coaches are fond of telling writers that they need to be sympathetic toward all their characters — minor characters, main characters, and even their villains. Without the author's sympathetic eye, characters become cardboard figures and readers lose interest both in the characters and in the story. We can usually find ways of caring about minor characters, at least enough to make them interesting. But the challenge often comes with offering something in the character of a really villainous villain that readers can identify with.

One way of developing a more sympathetic character, villain, or minor character is to sit down and imagine having a conversation with him or her. Do this in your journal and don't worry about whether or not it becomes part of the book. Imagine telling this person, "I know you have some redemptive purpose in this book, and I can imagine, also, that, however misguided, you have deep-seated personal reasons — perhaps very dark reasons — for doing what you are doing. Share with me the most secret inner promptings that drive you and would help me understand you." The answers may surprise you. Be as creative and insightful as you can be with your questions. Write down what your villain or minor character tells you. For now, don't be concerned about how this will or won't turn up in the book. Believe me, it will always make a difference in how you describe your character later, even if you never use exactly the same words or directly reuse any of what you've written in your journal. These "secret" conversations with your characters have tremendous power, even when they remain invisible to your readers.

# FROM PERSONAL EXPERIENCE TO LITERARY ARTIFACT

Artists and writers draw from their own life experiences to create their work. But rarely do they steal directly from life to make art. Even in writing a biography or a personal memoir, writers never quite capture on paper exactly what happened in real life. As author Philip Furia says in *As Time Goes By: Creating Biography*, even biographers must "resist the impulse to tell everything they have learned about their subject.... They need to find the story...buried under all of that information they've gathered." They look at the themes, tensions, and personal fantasies behind their experiences and pick out the parts that are universal, that will strike a special chord with their readers. They look behind the surface of what life has handed them. Here are some examples:

1. *Character composites.* Characters are created from a variety of people or situations the creative person has known. The artistic rendering of the cruel stepfather the artist suffered with in real life becomes a villain in a fantasy novel, or a mean boss in a young adult novel, and so on.

2.  *Transforming wounds.* Childhood wounds, such as humiliation and shame, that were never healed in real life form a story with a resolution when tormentor and victim become friends.

3.  *Rewriting tensions and conflicts.* We recall the emotional tension of a conflict we recently felt with a boss to reconstruct the tensions between children from two families who are brought under one roof in a second marriage.

4.  *Loss and grief.* In writing a story about a twelve-year-old child moving to another city, the author draws upon the memories of his grief at the death of his grandmother, allowing him to be very convincing in his writing about the child's feelings when he must leave his best friends behind.

5.  *Reframing plots and stories.* During a vacation adventure you take a guided tour through a cave and become very frightened. Later, you look at the fantasies of fear you had during that tour — that you would be trapped in a cave-in and be buried alive. A year or two later you write a compelling book about two children who are trapped in a cave and must rally all their courage and ingenuity to escape.

6.  *Themes.* How many times have you thought, or even heard yourself say, "I've learned my lesson about that!" Maybe it was about trusting someone

your instincts told you wasn't trustworthy. Maybe it was about putting off repairs on your car, or calling ahead for reservations, or something more serious than any of these. You can often find themes for stories in these life lessons. Look for them and weave them into a story.

7. *Personal interest.* Most successful writers will tell you that the best cure for writer's block is to start out with a concept or source of interest that you feel impassioned about. Set your stories in landscapes that excite you or bring you great pleasure in real life. Have your characters involved in vocations or avocations that intrigue you. Do you love the sea? Set your stories there. Have you always wanted to be a bush pilot in Alaska? Research it with a ride with such a pilot and build your story around that.

Always remember that your inner world is your greatest creative resource. Use it well.

*The great joy of the artist is to become aware
of a higher order of things, to recognize by the
compulsive and spontaneous manipulation of his
own impulses the resemblance between human
creation and what is called "divine" creation.*

## — HENRY MILLER

*HENRY MILLER ON WRITING*

# TRANSFORM YOUR INNER
# CRITICS INTO ALLIES

Most writers are plagued by inner critics, those *still, small but powerful voices* that speak from within, as if talking behind our backs, asking unsettling questions such as, "What makes you think you're a writer?" Or, "You're not a writer and you never will be. This is drivel. Don't waste your time." Or, the classic, "Get a day job. You'll never make a living this way." Everyone has these inner critics, though some of us find that their voices are louder or their criticisms more cutting than others. In their most insidious form, we feel these inner critics as our own self-judgments — in fact, judgments that are usually based on something that's recently happened to us. We write a few lines or pages that upon our review are just terrible. Instead of just rewriting or editing them, we point to them as evidence that we really can't write.

It's difficult to accept that these critics, who stop us in our creative tracks, are within us; they may have originated through events that happened in our past but today exist only in our minds. To free yourself of these inner critics' influences, you need to *own* them, fully acknowledge that you are creating them today. If you can own your inner critic, it means you have a choice — to cling to their judgments or not. But don't try to push them away; they will only grow stronger if you do, arguing like stubborn and willful children. You can *let them go*, that is, reduce your attachment to them. How? Start by making them characters in a story or in small vignettes that you write in your journal. Describe them in detail, the more detail the better: the color of their eyes, the color of their hair, their body type, their voice.

C. G. Jung encountered a form of inner critic in what he called the *animus*. His experience, reported in *Memories, Dreams, Reflections*, was that the animus, or inner critic, has its most powerful impact on our emotional life only when it remains unconscious and unnamed. As long as it is unconscious and unnamed, we experience it as inseparable from us. In fact, we can grow to feel quite attached to its harsh criticisms of us. He found that by "personifying" them we essentially "strip them of their power." They are still there in our psyches but we see them as separate from ourselves and thus can better take their harsh judgments with a grain of salt. As writers, we can even use them as prototypes for characters in stories.

Feel free to satirize your inner critics as characters separate from you. The more "real" you can make them on paper, the more you will see them as ... well, as characters with their own opinions. And you then have much more choice about accepting or rejecting what they say about you. Who knows, you may have just discovered a colorful character — or maybe just one aspect of a more sympathetic character — for your next story or article.

# DON'T FORGET: THE FIRST PERSON IS A CHARACTER, TOO!

The first-person voice — I, *me*, *my*, *mine*, and such — is most often associated with journal writing, memoirs, and autobiography, genres that traditionally convey truths about the author's own life experience. But when you're writing in the first person, don't forget that it takes more than a good tale to hold your readers' interest. The *character* telling the story will make the difference between enthralling your readers and putting them to sleep. So be sure that you put as much care into developing your first-person voice as you would into writing in the third person, from the point of view of a fictional character.

How do you create this sense of character if you are writing a memoir? After all, you're writing about yourself and your own experiences. Isn't your own personality going to come through? Won't that be character enough? Not necessarily. Unless you're a natural storyteller, you'll probably need to work on it. If you don't, the writing can easily become prosaic, a mere reportage of things that have happened to you. Great storytellers get good at what they do by carefully selecting experiences from their lives, and details of character, so that readers become intrigued not only by the events and experiences they describe but by how the story is delivered.

The "voice" for your first-person narrative, whether it's for a memoir or a fictional work, isn't *invented* so much as it's *discovered*. By that, I mean it comes not from *out there* but from *inside you*. You discover it by stepping back and observing your thoughts, actions, and feelings as the raw material for creating a character. What idiosyncrasies, quirks, doubts, fears, aspirations, or even physical traits would you describe if you were creating a fictional character based on what you know about yourself? What events and insights from your life might engage readers emotionally, intellectually, or spiritually? What character traits would you like to emphasize about yourself?

In her book *The Invitation*, a reflective memoir, the author Oriah Mountain Dreamer provides images that give us glimpses into her private moments of quiet reflection. In one scene, she tells about returning home after a party, feeling strangely unsettled by the superficiality of what she calls *social conversations*:

> *Restless, I sat down at my desk in the darkness and listened to the sounds around me gradually diminish as the city settled into sleep. There in the quiet, with the street lamp casting a pale light into the room, I picked up my pen and wrote what I really wanted to say to the people I had met that evening. . . .*

Oriah's narrative voice comes alive for us in these two lines. We see her sitting at her desk writing, a thoughtful and introspective person whose insights might help us in our own lives. It is easy for us to identify with her at that moment — sitting at her desk late at night, reflecting on what she had really wanted to say to the people at the party.

Bestselling essayist David Sedaris uses another technique to develop the character for his narrative voice. He describes himself in humorous, gently self-deprecating ways. For example, in telling about his eye for fashion — or his lack of it — he says, "The only expensive thing I actually wear is a navy blue cashmere sweater. It cost four hundred dollars and looks like it was wrestled from the mouth of a tiger." How much more these two sentences tell us about the narrator's character than had he merely said, "I sometimes wear an old navy blue cashmere sweater. It cost four hundred dollars."

Fiction writers offer some clues for taking that all-important step back from yourself to develop your narrative character. In Mark Twain's *The Adventures of Huckleberry Finn*, his first-person narrator, Huck, is a teenaged boy, a younger version of the middle-aged man Twain actually was at the time. To establish this narrator's voice, the author has Huck introduce himself by referring to the author's previous work: "You don't know about me without you have read a book by the name of *The Adventures of Tom Sawyer*." As if to have a little fun at Twain's expense, the young narrator tells us that this is "mostly a true book, with some stretchers." Having introduced Huck in this way, the author is careful to stay in character throughout, paying particular attention to Huck's own idioms and patterns of speech.

Another fiction writer, Leif Enger, starts his first-person novel with a story about his narrator that compels us to keep reading. *Peace Like a River* opens with this line: "From my first breath in this world, all I wanted was a good set of lungs." He tells how he was not breathing when he was born. He is alive to tell his story only because, at the last possible moment, his father rushed into the room, gathered the infant up in his arms, and demanded, "Reuben Land, in the name of the living God I am telling you to breathe." Whereupon he did.

Good first-person character development always helps to generate readers' *willing suspension of disbelief*, encouraging them to immerse themselves in the world you have created on the page. There's magic in leading readers across that psychic bridge between their world and yours ... and that magic begins with the attention you give to creating the character of your narrator.

Explore this process further by taking an entry from your journal or other private writing. Step back and pretend that what you've written are the thoughts and feelings of a character you are developing for a story. If it helps, make up a pseudonym for this character. Describe the person sitting down to write. Try adding self-observations, particularly ones about your own eccentricities and foibles. For example:

*In my twenties a friend suggested I try journal writing to work out what I considered earthshaking problems. Not that I was fool enough to believe I could actually solve the world's troubles that way. But I did find small comfort imagining I could at least unravel some of my own tangles.*

Experiment with humor. There's nothing like poking a little fun at yourself to evoke readers' sympathy, assuring them that you're nothing if not humble. In her book *Small Wonder*, Barbara Kingsolver reflects on feelings she had in her teenage years: "I am too awkward and quiet behind my curtain of waist-length hair, a girl unnoticed, a straight-A schoolmouse who can't pass for dumb and cute in a small-town, marry-young market that values — as far as I can see — no other type." Kingsolver's humor reminds us that teenage angst is, after all, pretty universal and forgivable. But more than that, it offers us a charming, if somewhat cranky, character that we can easily identify with.

Well-written first-person narrative is intimate, giving readers the impression that you are speaking directly to them. This is true whether the author is the narrator — as with Sedaris, Kingsolver, and Mountain Dreamer — or the narrator is a fictional character created by the author — as with Twain's Huck and Enger's Reuben. The success of good writing, be it fact or fiction, depends as much on the character of the teller as on what's being told. Take the time to develop your first-person narrator's character and your writing will sing, capturing the hearts and minds of your readers.

*I write entirely to find out what I'm thinking,
what I'm looking at, what I see and what it means.
What I want and what I fear.*

— **JOAN DIDION**

IN *THE WRITER AND HER WORK,*
EDITED BY JANET STERNBURG

# WELCOME YOUR MUSE

As writers, we don't always appreciate the source of our creative inspiration. Some artists say don't question that source or try to figure it out, for you'll surely chase it away. Like the characters you create in a story or the creative way you develop an essay or work of nonfiction, your muse is the product of billions of brain cells interacting from both hemispheres of your brain. Although the creative process is still a great mystery to science, experience indicates that when we get too analytical or calculated in our efforts, we probably do inhibit that process. Most authors and artists talk about welcoming the muse, not by exerting great effort but by preparing a space for it in our inner lives, then letting go and being receptive to what it offers. I like the quote by bestselling author Lynn V. Andrews (*Medicine Woman*), "Creativity is like a great receptive womb."

Who or what is the muse that inspires *your* creativity? It might be an imaginary person, a figure who arose in your consciousness spontaneously. It could be a mythological figure, a historical character, a real person from your past, or a person who is presently in your life. But it need not be a person. It might be an animal or a mystical being such as an angel or a sphere of light. Indigenous peoples from every continent share traditions of calling upon *spirit animals* for storytelling and wisdom seeking. Your muse might be an inspiring *place* that you visit in your mind — even, yes, an image that represents a receptive womb. I've known several authors who reported that when they wanted to get their creative energies flowing, they imagined themselves in a cave, usually one with a shaft of sunlight illuminating their writing space and where they also imagined having all the modern conveniences at their disposal.

One of my own favorite muse places is a small garden studio that I built many years ago. I no longer own the property and have not visited it in many years. The structure may have even been torn down long ago, for all I know, but this tiny studio still lives in my mind's eye. I have only to imagine myself in this space and my creativity is energized. It is as vivid in my memory as images of my childhood home and some of my favorite vacation spots.

Muses have inspired writers for as long as there have been scribblers and storytellers. Most people know about William Blake (1757–1827), of course, who commented that his poem "Jerusalem" was literally dictated to him by his muse. Less well known is the experience of Napoleon Hill (1883–1970), businessman and author of the best-selling book *Think and Grow Rich*, who had his "inner counsel of advisors." This "council" included Ralph Waldo Emerson, Thomas Paine, Thomas Edison, Charles Darwin, Abraham Lincoln, Napoleon Bonaparte, and

Andrew Carnegie. These were all men with qualities Hill admired and wanted to emulate. He studied them through their biographies and other writings and imagined each of them, as one might do for characters in a novel — or, more precisely, how they were in real life. Hill would bring them all into an imaginary round table discussion, where they debated one another and engaged in lively repartee that covered many subjects and inspired Hill's own work.

The author Alice Walker reports that when she was writing her novel *The Color Purple* she frequently engaged her characters — Celie, Shug, and others — in imaginary dialogues. She would sit down even when she was not actively writing and talk with her characters. They became very real to her, and in this way, Shug and the others served dual roles, as both muses and characters for her writing.

A clear mental picture of your muse — whether it's a person, a group of people, a place, a thing, an animal, or perhaps just a state of mind — provides an important reference point in your consciousness, one that can provide an increasingly compelling charge of inspiration the more you use it. Just as images of success focus your efforts to achieve important personal goals, so these imaginings can focus your heart and mind, preparing that special place in your consciousness, the receptive womb Lynn Andrews describes.

Whenever you are on a creative roll, pause for a moment and explore whatever or whomever comes to your mind to represent or symbolize this experience for you. Get in touch with your feelings about the experience and embody them with the metaphor, image, or memory that most vividly describes those feelings. You can then bring them to mind whenever you wish to move deeper into that special state of consciousness where you do your best writing. Think of this as a *welcoming* process, making a comfortable space in your mind for your muse to truly come alive for you.

# HOME AGAIN

Imagine that you have returned to your childhood home after many years away. Has anything changed? Observe the activity in the streets, the surrounding landscape, even natural phenomena that you once took very much for granted, believing they would never change. Imagine walking or driving past the house or other buildings or even the countryside where you lived. Maybe you go inside the house where you grew up, or where you spent much of your time as a child. Imagine visiting a public place such as a coffee shop, a grocery, a teen hangout, a church where a friend was married, an athletic field, or a school. You find that while seeing it again brings up a great many memories, good and bad, it may have changed so significantly that you barely recognize it. Perhaps the property has aged and is suffering from neglect. Or maybe it has been beautifully maintained or remodeled in such a way that you feel your memories of the place have been erased. Put yourself into this scene: describe the changes you presently see and compare them to the past, weaving into these descriptions your own past experiences, either as a child or later in your life. What feelings do you experience in this journey into the past?

As you relive the past, try doing so from the perspective of the person you were at the time, many years younger than you are today, taking into account factors such as the size of your body, your youth, your relative innocence about the world, the rhythms of your body and of the world around you, the tone of your voice, what scared you when you lived in this place, what brought you joy, how you found peace or solace when you were sad or depressed or simply bewildered.

Let any images and feelings inspire you to go into longer descriptions of people from your past and what they meant to you when you were younger and what they mean to you now. Explore key events that changed you, such as the end of childhood and beginning of adolescence, having a friend or family member move away or die. Tell about a pet you had when you were young, feelings and beliefs associated with your childhood that may or may not have changed. Are there any unresolved feelings — regrets, injuries, losses, old jealousies, mysteries, fears — that are stirred up by this imaginary journey into the past? Are there hopes or dreams that are reawakened? Write about them at whatever depth you wish.

*The story — from* Rumplestiltskin *to*
War and Peace *— is one of the basic tools
invented by the human mind, for the purpose
of gaining understanding. There have been great
societies that did not use the wheel, but there
have been no societies that did not tell stories.*

— **URSULA K. LE GUIN**
"PROPHETS AND MIRRORS,"
IN *THE LIVING LIGHT*

# WRITING A GREAT STORY
# SIMPLIFIED

Most people read fiction, memoirs, creative nonfiction, and biographies not just for information or entertainment but because they enjoy imagining how it would be to live in a world different from their own. How would it feel? What would it look like? What would we hear, smell, and taste? There may be a time in history, a situation, people, or knowledge your readers closely identify with, or at least are curious about, and that's important. But if you want to deeply engage them, you must remember that we all live in a finite, physical world and find our way around it through our senses — sight, sound, touch, taste, and smell. The more you can give your reader sensory cues, the more they will be able to come with you into the world, actual or fictional, that you're creating in your mind.

I'm exaggerating in the following examples for the sake of making my point, but which of the two descriptions — number 1 or number 2 — gives you the more vivid sense of being transported into a world different from your own?

Example 1: *I was escorted into a large room where I sat down in a big green chair.*

Example 2: *A man wearing a bright blue blazer with shiny brass buttons met me at the brick and wrought iron entrance of 965 Ivy Way. He nodded when I showed him my invitation, then bowed, inserted an oversized key into the lock of the wide red door, then held it open as I stepped over the threshold. I walked into a high-ceilinged foyer with a floor of lovely Italian tile, almost missing the discreet little sign that said, "Please remove your shoes." I sat down on a padded leather bench provided for this purpose, removed my shoes, and placed them in one of the cubbyholes built into the wall to the right of the bench. Beyond the foyer was a white-carpeted room the size of a high school auditorium. It was empty except for twelve green velvet chairs arranged in a perfect circle at the center. I was obviously the first to arrive. I crossed the room, feeling the plush carpeting under my stocking feet, selected one of the chairs, and sat down as my host had instructed in a phone message earlier in the day.*

Notice how the detailed description of the entrance to the room, the room itself, and what the narrator does there helps us to create, in our own minds, a sense of entering a world quite different from our own. As a reader, can you help but be curious about what's going to happen next or why anyone would have a room like this? Notice the sensory information that helps to create this illusion of entering a different world: the doorman's uniform, the wrought iron and brick entrance, the wide red door, the tiled entrance, the expansive carpeted room with the twelve chairs in a circle. All of these details help to transport the reader into this imaginary world.

Use the same techniques for describing characters, whether you are writing fictional characters, anecdotes about a real person, a memoir, or a biography. Look for physical characteristics that help your readers create a mental picture of the character. Compare the two following descriptions:

Example 3: *Bart was a handsome, athletic man in his thirties.*

Example 4: *When Bart entered a room, people sat up and took notice. Six feet eight inches tall, wearing tailored jeans and a white, freshly pressed dress shirt, open at the collar, his athletic physique exuded the sensuality and litheness of a panther. Something about his smile betrayed a faintly concealed aura of danger, even as his intelligent brown eyes and quick smile confirmed that he was supremely at ease with himself.*

Again, notice how much the details not only tell us about the man's physical presence and what he's wearing but also suggest something about his personality and how other people relate to him. The details of this description set the mood for any scene that might follow, all with seventy-two words.

## Dialogue: Don't Be Too Real

One of the best things I learned in creative writing school was to keep dialogue sparse. Leave out the obvious. Try not to copy real-life conversation, because if you do it'll come off sounding fake.

> Example 5: *Maisey stood up and greeted George with a hug. "So, how are you, George?" she asked. "Fine," he said, returning the hug warmly. "And how about you?"*
>
> *"I'm good," Maisey said. "Make yourself comfortable. It's been a long time since we last got together like this. I'm so glad you came."*

> Example 6: *They exchanged greetings, then Maisey threw her arms around George and buried her head in his shoulder. "I'm so glad to see you," she said.*

Most of the dialogue in example 5 is empty verbiage. The back-and-forth greetings of the two characters tell us very little about either the characters or the scene. What's important here is that two friends are meeting and are glad to see each other. That's established quickly in example 6 through narrative, with Maisey's hug and a single line of dialogue. Sort out what's necessary or unnecessary for the dialogue by asking yourself what purpose it serves to move along your story.

## Writing Between the Lines

Have you ever noticed that dialogue can reveal as much in the *spaces between the lines* as in what's actually said? It can reveal how much or how little people are listening to each other. Or how they are avoiding any real connection with one another. Or that there's a tension building between them. For example, notice the following exchange between a mother and her twenty-something daughter who has just shown up hours late for a family dinner:

*"I've been so worried about you, Ashley. Where have you been?"*

*"I know it's late, Mom. I hope I didn't spoil things."*

*"Annette was so disappointed. She was looking forward to seeing you! Tell me you weren't with Carlos again."*

*"Oh, god, I'm so starved I could even eat your overcooked broccoli and rice."*

*"Don't criticize my cooking, dear. I do my best."*

*"I know you do. I'm sorry."*

> *"He's so beneath you, darling."*
> *"Beneath me, above me! I hope you saved me some dinner."*

Notice how the daughter skirts her mother's questions about Carlos. She avoids answering directly, changes subjects, even digs at her mother about her cooking. Ashley is manipulative, her mother passive and codependent, trying to make things okay but obviously disturbed by her daughter's behavior. Eight short lines of dialogue paint a picture of two characters and the tension between them, established as much by what's not said as by what is.

Practice writing dialogue like this, where what isn't said is at least as important as what is.

## Lost in Time: Present Intents

The main body of every good story takes place within a certain time period. Boy meets girl in 1978 and struggles to win her love for the next five years until, in 1983, they are finally married. That's what I refer to as the *real time* of the story. This doesn't mean you can't go outside this time frame. For example, you might briefly visit a time from a character's past. You might go back to 1968 when the boy first met the girl at a football game. But be careful you don't get so wrapped up in telling about that first meeting that you take the reader outside the real-time portion of the story. If you do, they may very well be confused. They'll consciously or unconsciously start asking, "Wait, where is this story going? What's the author doing here?" And when that happens, most readers are going to put the book down, skip pages until they come back to real time, or plough through with the reading without enjoying it. In fact, they might get quite irritated with the author, and you don't want that to happen because word of mouth is the main thing that sells books.

Just as you want to be careful about taking readers too far into the past, you also don't want to take them too quickly into the future. The future unfolds gradually in real time — in the period from 1978 to 1983, in this case. Glimpsing the future is called *foreshadowing*, and in most writers' minds that's a no-no. It's the equivalent of a comedian telling the punch line before the story. For example, take a look at the following:

*Maisey left the meeting with George that day feeling good about him. Perhaps they'd crossed a threshold into greater mutual trust. He had definitely changed. She was sure of it. As difficult as it had been his love was once more confirmed. Only months later would she discover that she had been sadly and cruelly betrayed.*

In most cases foreshadowing undermines subtle tensions that keep readers wanting to know what happens next. While there's tension in the dark foreboding of the last sentence in the previous example, the writer sacrifices the reader's desire to trust George and believe, as Maisey does, that he has really changed and everything is going to be okay.

## Putting It All Together

Don't understand this material too quickly. These are core principles of storytelling condensed into a single short reading. Check it out against what you already know, or use it as a touchstone to come back to from time to time. As with all advice about the creative process, the rules are meant to be challenged. But it's best to know what those rules are before you shatter them.

*To have one's individuality completely ignored
is like being pushed quite out of life. Like
being blown out as one blows out a light.*

— **EVELYN SCOTT**
*ESCAPADE*

# FOLLOW YOUR PASSIONS

Take a moment to reflect on the passions that motivate you to write. What is the driving force that causes you to pick up your journal or sit down at your computer to record a certain idea or experience? Perhaps your passion is to write about certain people, famous or not so famous. Perhaps your passion is self-knowledge. Or maybe there are historical events or personal milestones that inspire you. Is your passion a message you wish to share with others?

The great southern writer Eudora Welty said, "Passion is our ground, our island — do others exist?"

Spend some time writing about what you most want to share with your readers. Ask yourself how you would like your readers to be affected by your writing. What would you like them to know? What actions would you like them to take after reading what you have written? Or, simply, what state of mind and heart would you want them to experience during and after reading your work?

It may be that you write not for others but only for yourself. Is this, in fact, the source of your passion? If so, get in touch with what it is in yourself that is served through your writing. What is satisfied or stimulated? Do you feel expanded by what you write, more centered or whole? Do you feel a sense of relief, freedom, or even ecstasy?

Let what is in your heart speak for you, then give this voice room to expand and fill your imagination. This is how you find your ground.

*Writing is a kind of double living. The writer experiences everything twice. Once in reality and once in that mirror which waits always before or behind.*

— **CATHERINE DRINKER BOWEN**
IN *THE ATLANTIC*

# WHERE CHARACTERS ARE BORN

Drawing from your own life experience, you will discover everything you need to create original and exciting characters. Whether you draw from memories of people who were or are close to you in your everyday life or from mythological figures, all can be invaluable resources. Stephen King once said that some of his characters were based on his own worst nightmares, while Edna O'Brien said simply, "We have so many voices in us, how do we know which ones to obey?"

Most great characters in literature are borrowed from real life. Borrow the way one person walks or laughs. Combine these traits with the intellectual capacities of another. Mix those qualities with the lifestyle of still another person — the quick-wittedness or melancholy or callousness or compassion of another. Mix and match! As you synthesize the character traits in ways that please you and serve specific purposes in your story, they will take on lives of their own, be unlike any person in real life, ultimately expressing your own inimitable *voice*.

If you are creating anecdotes for nonfiction, use a similar process, changing aspects of a real person, such as gender and age, to disguise the real person involved or to honor the privacy of a particular client, patient, friend, relative, or acquaintance while still providing a clear illustration of an insight you want to share with your readers.

In the process of creating a character, we're not always sure where our models come from. For example, there's a certain character — I'll call him Darrel — who turns up in several stories I've written. My model for him reaches far back in my youth. He's a friend from my teen years. I lived for the outdoors in those days, and he was the ultimate outdoorsman. I hunted and fished, like Darrel, primarily because it gave me a reason to spend time outside. Believe me, in the dead of winter, with three feet of snow covering the ground, you need a good excuse to tromp around in the woods, and hunting was how one justified such insanity in the rural area of Michigan where I grew up. In the middle of summer, with temperature and humidity hovering in the nineties, and with clouds of mosquitoes infesting the air, it was equally difficult to rationalize why you were outdoors...except to cast a fly for trout.

My friend Darrel was seven years my senior. He had dropped out of school before he learned to read, mainly, I think, because his schoolmates tormented him for his physical handicap. He had a withered left arm, half the length of his other, with a hand that appeared fairly normal except it was more like a four-year-old child's. As far as I could tell, this anomaly didn't get in the way of hunting, fishing, or his other activities. He was an equally good shot with a rifle or shotgun, handled a fly rod well, and as far as I know never used his imperfection as an avoidance excuse.

He knew which bait to use for bass, which for trout, how to track deer, where to find rabbits or pheasant, as well as the legal seasons for all. (He also possessed an uncanny ability for eluding the game warden when procuring meat was more urgent than compliance with the law.) When not fishing or hunting he worked as a handyman and semiskilled laborer for a few dollars an hour and was a decent wood finisher. Both my parents — my father an engineer, my mother a schoolteacher — were bewildered by my friendship with him. Their bewilderment turned to distress, and maybe horror, when they discovered he'd been arrested a few times, mostly for being drunk and disorderly. They did not know that in his teens he'd been arrested for breaking into a gas station and stealing $38 and a case of Milky Way candy bars.

What I recall about Darrel from real life has made its way into a number of other characters in stories I've written. For example, one of the things that inspired me about him was his ability not just to triumph over his physical handicap but seemingly to be *almost* unaware of it. That same trait — let's call it "conscious unawareness" — has turned up in characters who overcame other kinds of challenges, such as what should have been emotionally crippling childhoods, or maybe intellectual limitations. As earthy and simple as Darrel was in real life, he was also living proof of the transcendent for me. If not a saint, he was simply proof of man's ability to — in William Faulkner's words — "not only to endure but to prevail."

As an exploration in character development, take the qualities of three people you know and create a composite character that is not quite like any of them.

# LONELY ROAD

You are driving to visit a friend in the country. It is during the evening hours and the sun is just going down. You are on a remote back road — a shortcut your friend has told you about over the phone. Imagine the landscape in any way you wish, whether forest or prairie, desert, mountains, or farmland. You slow slightly for a long, sweeping turn and see a child you're sure can't be more than seven or eight, hitchhiking at the side of the road. You cannot at first be certain if it is a boy or a girl. You brake to slow slightly so that you can get a better look.

The child has long hair that tumbles out from under a hat of some kind — perhaps a baseball hat, a knit cap, a skully, or even something more curious, such as a bowler or top hat. (This could be an opportunity to use your description of the hat and other articles of clothing to pique the readers' curiosity.)

This young person also carries a backpack. Again, you might play with the description of the pack to excite readers' interest. Maybe it's a large pack that seems like a great burden, or it's an odd color, or it is decorated in an unusual way. This person smiles as you approach, maybe raises a hand to wave, but since it has never been your habit to pick up hitchhikers, you step on the accelerator and drive on.

You might portray yourself as having many fears cross your mind. Maybe this innocent-looking child is just a decoy. Maybe an adult with less innocent intentions is hiding nearby. You decide not to chance it. You drive past.

As you watch in the rearview mirror, however, nobody else appears and the child seems to watch longingly after your car. You finally stop, make a U-turn, and head back toward the hitchhiking child. Stopping on the opposite side of the road, you swing the door open and call to them. The child jogs across the road and thanks you, and you get out to help them load their backpack into the trunk.

What happens next? Who is the child? Where is he or she going? What's the outcome of this event?

# SNAPSHOTS IN TIME

You are driving through a town hundreds of miles from your home. You stop for gasoline or to get some lunch, then drive around and explore the new territory. In your travels you pass a sign advertising a neighborhood garage sale and decide to visit it. Though this is something you rarely do, you are feeling adventurous and lucky. Maybe in this town that you didn't even realize existed, you'll discover an unexpected treasure.

You drive up to where the garage sale is taking place and park your car. A dozen or more tables are set up in someone's driveway, displaying the usual castoffs from people's lives — paperback books, a couple of old lamps, toaster ovens, barbeque tools still in their original box, a cardboard carton full of canning jars at 25 cents apiece, a framed paint-by-numbers picture of a log cabin near a babbling stream, some rusty hand tools....

You wander around and spot a stack of old framed pictures. You idly start going through them, in search of a decent-looking frame for some photographs you have at home. In the process, you come upon a photo of a handsome young man (or woman) and your heart skips a beat. You are absolutely certain that this is a photo of an ex-lover whom you have not seen for many years. You stand there holding the picture, staring at it, then notice something written at the bottom. It is addressed to some other person, not a name you recognize or that rings any bells for you. And then there's the inscription, with some flowery love saying at the end, and this dedication: "To the most important person who has ever come into my life." The signature is definitely that of your ex.

Describe your experience in that moment. What did you feel and think? What memories — good, bad, or indifferent — were aroused? Take the story as far as you wish. Did you ask any of the people tending the tables about the photograph? What did you find out, if anything, about why the photograph was there? Did you buy the photograph and take it home? Did this discovery lead to any further actions, such as a reunion of old friends? Or did you meet with the person in the photo and tell them what you really thought of them? Finish this exercise, as best you can, with a sense of having completed unfinished business from the original breakup with the person in the picture.

# THE QUESTION IS...

In her book *At Seventy*, May Sarton said, "I have never written a book that was not born out of a question I needed to answer for myself." Many other authors have shared similar thoughts. Indira Gandhi said, "The power to question is the basis of all human progress." And let's not forget the riddle of the Sphinx. In Greek mythology, the Sphinx sat outside the city of Thebes and asked this question of every traveler who passed by: "What goes on four legs in the morning, two legs at noon, and three legs in the evening?" If travelers gave the wrong answer, they paid with their lives. If they answered correctly, the Sphinx destroyed herself. In Sophocles' *Oedipus Rex*, arguably one of the greatest plays of all time, Oedipus answered correctly and the Sphinx, indeed, destroyed herself. (*Answer:* Humans. We crawl on all fours as babies, walk on two legs as adults, and walk with a cane in old age.)

Inherent in every mystery novel is the question, *Whodunit?* In virtually every nonfiction book, there's a question or series of questions that the author seeks to answer:

- What is it like to travel to such-and-such a place?

- How can I best handle this life problem or that?

- Why did the biographical subject do what he or she did?

- What should I expect when I'm expecting?

- How can I lose thirty pounds?

And what makes the proverbial *page turner*, the book that keeps you reading way past midnight? It's your curiosity, questions that the best authors keep inspiring in you:

- And then what happened?

- What's the rest of the story?

- How did they do that?

- What were they feeling and thinking?

- What else should I know about this?

There have been whole books written about the power of questions. Marilee Adams's bestselling book *Change Your Questions, Change Your Life* — which I had the privilege of working on with the author — begins with the main character describing a plaque on his desk that reads, "Great results begin with great questions." The whole book explores the power of questions.

The energy of the creative process perhaps always gets started with the question, *What if?* Or, *Why did this happen?* Or, of course, *Whodunit?*

In your journal, list at least three questions that might motivate you to write a particular story or a nonfiction work of any length. Whatever your questions, state them as clearly and simply as you can.

Questions help to focus our attention. They might involve seeking the solution to a crime you have heard about. You might have questions about a certain relationship in your life, the peculiar motives of someone you've known or met. They might explore how you could have handled a difficult situation more skillfully. You might have questions about emotional, spiritual, or religious experiences. Maybe you want to explore questions you have about a specific time in history, or about the lives of people who lived during a certain period.

After listing your questions, start elaborating on them in any way that comes to mind. This might involve reliving the events when you first became aware of the questions, how you might express one or more of them in a short story, article, or book, profiles of any people involved, your thoughts and feelings about your questions right now, and so on.

Take your time and leave room in your journal to revisit these questions in the future. The more sharply focused and refined your questions, the sharper you'll be able to concentrate your readers' attention, and the more eager they will be to read what you have to say. Good questions are the seeds from which every book-worthy idea grows.

# CHECKLIST FOR
# CREATING CHARACTERS

1. Choose characters' names so that readers can easily keep them straight — instead of Dan and David, which are easy to mix up, try Dan and Arnold. Some authors make sure that all their characters' names start with a different letter.

2. Name your characters fittingly: "Bruno," a bearlike man; "Tina," a petite young woman; "Marshall," a tough cop. Add another dimension by having the character's personal attributes contradict his or her name: "Tina," a female body builder more than six feet tall; "Bruno," a wiry male ballet dancer; "Marshall," a sensitive masseuse.

3. Give careful thought to physical characteristics and capacities. Will it help your story if your character is physically strong? Right- or left-handed? Tall or short? Handsome or ugly? How might a character's identifying birthmark, infirmity, or scar help the story?

4. What's the socioeconomic background of each character, and in what ways does that background explain something about his or her behavior, motivations, strengths, weaknesses, or the power that others have over him or her or that he or she has over others?

5. The gender of each character is important, of course, but don't be afraid to *bend* genders, such as featuring a female race car driver, or a male who is a nurturing stay-at-home parent, or an ex-fashion model who is a heartless, hard-driving CEO.

6. When writing dialogue, play with speech patterns that help to identify characters and their backgrounds: precise and perfect grammar for a priggish college professor type; coarse language, contractions, and faulty grammar for a circus roustabout. Use dialects very sparingly unless you really know them well.

7. Consider using your characters' living arrangements to help define them. Why does the attractive forty-year-old woman live with her mother? How can the young couple afford a fancy vacation home? Why is the sixty-year-old doctor living in a rundown trailer park?

8. What thoughts and feelings does each character have about each other character? Is Dorothy secretly in love with her husband's father? Is Jack

secretly plotting to embezzle a million dollars and throw the blame on the stepbrother he hates?

9. How might you use your characters' beliefs to create conflict? For example, the pro-labor son of a conservative businessman tries to unionize his father's factory; a pro-life activist's daughter begs for an abortion after her brutal rape; a young farmer goes up against his three brothers' wishes to sell the family property.

10. How might ethnic differences, cultural backgrounds, or nationality help to define your characters? Always make certain these details are integral to the story; otherwise readers may feel you are being disingenuous.

11. Take your readers into your characters' private inner worlds to reveal their longings, dreams, nightmares. Use this information to show disparities between your characters' inner truths and outward behavior.

12. Make sure you understand what each character is doing in your book. How does each one move your story forward? What is his or her impact on other characters — particularly the main ones? Do readers need more information, or less, about any of your characters?

# THE FINE ART OF OBSERVATION

Writers are nothing if not observers of life. We may think of ourselves as innovators, as having the ability to describe things in a creative way that causes our readers to sit up and take notice. Surely our crafting of words is integral to our art, but *observing* is a skill too often overlooked. In our role as observer we quiet our minds and give our senses an opportunity to take in what's there without projecting too much of our own meaning. Only then, with an openness to new possibilities, might we notice the patterns of the autumn light between the shadows of the apple tree's branches. Only then might we hear the click of the old dog's claws as he slowly crosses the kitchen floor, or recognize the faint scent of a friend's perfume as she enters the room. Only then might we feel the warm breeze on the back of our necks as the front door is eased open in the hallway behind us.

If we're writing a scene for a story, these fine observations provide us with the kinds of details that transport our readers out of their everyday world into the world we're creating on paper. But where do these little nuances come from? Through careful observation, even tiny details take up residence in our consciousness, hiding out in the shadowy recesses of memory until we need them. When we're doing the writing we may be nowhere near the room or landscape we're describing. Rather, we construct these details by drawing upon memories of our previous observations — even from experiences that date back years or decades.

How much time does any of us spend really observing — seeing, hearing, tasting, smelling, feeling? Instead of pausing to witness, we try to make sense of the world. Our minds are constantly in motion. Someone says, *Look at the shadows on the patio*; we quickly reply, *Oh, yes, that's the branches of the apple tree*. We identify and label what we see, giving only fleeting attention to the odd patterns of light between the shadows cast by the branches. We hear the sound of the dog's claws on the floor and immediately think, *Oh, it's time to feed Fido*. We get up and feed the dog, and that's the end of it. Those quick responses can obliterate the patterns of the sunlight or the quality of the sounds the dog's claws make on the tile floor.

In conversations with a friend, we wait for him or her to pause so that we can say our piece, or we look for ideas we can respond to, either agreeing or disagreeing, depending on the subject or our frame of mind. But how often do we hear the qualities of other people's voices — *really* hear them — the cadence of their language, tiny traces of accents or inflections, where the sounds seem to come from, their chest, their neck, the back of their throat? It is our awareness of these subtle details that provides the raw materials for writings that grab our readers' attention, engage their minds, and keep them coming back for more.

Here are four guidelines for honing your abilities as an observer:

1. *Be silent.* Most of us are intimidated by silence. We immediately look for ways to fill the void by playing music, talking, or filling the silence with our own thoughts. Allow yourself to be a silent witness, minimizing your personal impact on the moment.

2. *Be curious.* Meet the world around you with inquisitiveness rather than explaining, interpreting, analyzing, telling, or even exclaiming. Be *in wonder* rather than seeking to know or understand. Let your thoughts begin and end with a question mark. Remember Albert Einstein's words: "There are only two ways to live your life. One is as though nothing is a miracle, the other is as though everything is a miracle."

3. *Be accepting.* Make no judgments about what's going on or what's said. For now just take in whatever the experience may be. Be discerning — don't stand in harm's way — but for the moment suspend all judgments of good/bad, wise/naive, beautiful/ugly, skilled/bumbling, innocent/knowledgeable. If you are tempted to *figure it out*, stop. Don't even try. Let it be as it is.

4. *Be open.* Let go of the everyday attraction to *know-ing* — to thinking, interpreting, giving your opinions, or even carrying on an inner dialogue about a certain issue in your life. Open your mind to new and different possibilities. If you find yourself looking at shadows, shift your focus to the light between or behind the shadows. If you tend to focus on the beauty of the rose, focus instead on the sculpted beauty of the thorn. If you tend to focus on the meaning of your friend's words, focus instead on the tonal qualities of his voice.

You will find that the more time you spend experiencing the world from the *witnessing* awareness of your observer self, the more you will discover yourself opening to the unexpected. You will discover what you didn't know and maybe never even imagined. We tend to look at the world through a narrow lens, one that allows us to see primarily only that which is most familiar to us, that which doesn't offend or frighten or embarrass us. While the narrow lens allows us to be more comfortable in our lives, it also limits our experiences, blinding us not just to what we might not want to see but to subtle nuances that can be the source of insight and even joy. The entomologist finds an amazingly collaborative community of insects in a clump of rotting matter; a woman who fears heights writes an article about paragliding and discovers the joys of flight; a man who struggled with gender identity as a teenager looks more openly at his fears and challenges them by taking up knitting, which he'd always thought of as effeminate. He discovers he loves it and turns it into a serious hobby, creating sweaters of his own design for both sexes.

The observer self allows us to see with new eyes and hear with new ears, offering new possibilities and new connections in our brains. We realize that we can be open, if only for brief glimpses, beyond the limits of our own comfort zones. We see details — colors, tones, textures, movements, even humor and intimacies — that were there all along, revealing themselves to us through our increased patience and openness. This observational capacity may very well hold the heart of creativity, from which come the imagery, language rhythms, metaphors, and insights that make writing so exciting and captivate our readers.

# SOLITUDE AND CREATIVITY

The creative process requires that you leave the external world and go to your private inner one. And while you dwell in this inner space, you don't want to be distracted by the external world. A telephone ringing, a spouse rushing into the room in search of the car keys or the grocery list, a child shrieking in your ear demanding your attention — all these jerk you out of the private reality that is the writer's life source. These are not just simple interruptions. When you are thoroughly immersed in your creative work they can feel like assaults, breaches of intimate boundaries.

Solitude contains and nurtures your inner world. It is here that we best access our self and the wealth of resources it holds. For most of us it's the only place where we dare be fully ourselves. Flannery O'Connor once said, "I am never more completely myself than when I am writing."

Think of solitude not as just a mood or sentiment but as your entrance to the imaginative theater where you project the illusions of sailing on the open sea, or taking a leisurely walk through a mountain village, or driving along city streets teeming with life, or sitting contentedly at home in your favorite chair. Solitude is where your mind opens to new possibilities and the currents of your creativity flow freely.

Write about ways that solitude works for you. Where do you go to find it? How do you feel when it is interrupted? Familiarize yourself with the ways it works in your life and how it serves your creative life. Examine ways you can protect it and have more of it in your life.

*My closely guarded solitude causes some
hurt feelings now and then. But how to explain,
without wounding someone, that you want to be
wholly in the world you are writing about, that
it would take two days to get the visitor's voice
out of the house so that you could listen to
your own characters again?*

— **MARGARET BOURKE-WHITE**
*PORTRAIT OF MYSELF*

# WRITERS' DREAMS

Take a few minutes to write about your wildest fantasies regarding what it might be like to become a really famous author. Write this in the first person, resisting any temptation you might have to limit yourself. This is your own private fantasy, so you can create anything you wish.

Focus on how you feel and what you do as you sit down to write each day after you have become this famous author. Tell how you feel upon the completion of your latest book, of what you experience when the book has been published and you hold the first copy in your hand. Describe how you'd feel reading a glowing review of your book appearing on an influential blog or in an important magazine. You might want to describe being interviewed for radio or national TV or perhaps for a magazine, or being recognized by a stranger, or asked for an autograph while sitting in a restaurant or other public place. Describe what it's like to be signing books for a long line of fans in a bookstore.

Come back to this dream from time to time to reawaken your excitement about becoming a published author. It's not only a fun writing exercise but an effective self-affirmation.

There's still another part of this: Some writers discover that being a bestselling author is not all it's cracked up to be. There's the loss of privacy, new demands on your time, and a certain role strangers expect you to fulfill. Publishers, as well as your readers, may not want you to stray much in future works from what's proved successful for you in the past. At such times, I'm told, you start recreating those illusions from when you were still a struggling writer — fantasizing about life as a bestseller.

# COLUMBO'S NOTEBOOK

You may remember or have seen reruns of the TV detective series *Columbo*, in which a middle-aged Peter Falk plays a rumpled detective, his trademarks a frayed trench coat and a twenty-year-old Peugeot convertible with fading paint and a threadbare canvas top. With his curious smile, the cigar-smoking Columbo often appeared confused, absentminded, a little slow, sometimes charming, yet maddeningly relentless in his pursuit of wrongdoers. His fans, of course, knew that his disarming manners concealed the keen observational abilities of a shrewd and seasoned criminologist. He never failed to get his man — or woman, as the case may be.

In nearly every episode Columbo had to borrow a pen from one of his suspects because he had forgotten or lost his own. Even so, he always had his little notebook for recording clues that he collected, though he usually had to search through several pockets before he found it. It was one of the cheap spiral-bound kind, as inconsequential as Columbo himself. That tiny notebook got my attention. I thought this would be the ideal notebook for writers. It could be whipped out in an instant to jot down a gem of insight, an image, or a line of dialogue overheard in a café.

I've had many fancy notebooks, even nice leather-bound ones with gold-edged papers and electronic ones that you write in with a stylus. But as often as not, when I most wanted them out in the field, I found I'd left them at home on my desk or couldn't read the screen in the sun. Besides, carrying around those fancy leather-bound ones always made me feel like a Bible salesman.

Legend has it that Hemingway liked those Moleskine notebooks, neat little books of 150 or so blank or ruled pages, measuring 3 x 5 inches and a half-inch thick. You can still buy them and they're very nice, with their soft suede covers. I had one but always worried about scratching up the covers or bending pages when I jammed it into my pocket with my car keys and change. So it usually got left at home.

It seems like those buck-and-a-half spiral-bound note-books are always there, in one pocket or another — though their pages may be dog-eared and bent. Tattered or not, they still serve the function they're designed for, and for this writer that's what matters most.

But there's yet another advantage these little scratch-pads have to offer. People rarely ask why you're writing in them, the way they sometimes do when you write in the fancier ones. That's a privacy factor worth considering. Good insurance against a stranger's awkward questions about what you're writing, where you've published, what your books are about, and . . . well, you get the picture.

I've decided that the unobtrusiveness and availability of a notebook are what most matter to me. The humbler it is the more likely it will be there when I need it — and I can usually borrow a pen.

*Writers do not live one life, they live two.*
*There is the living and then there is the*
*writing. There is the second tasting,*
*the delayed reaction.*

**— ANAÏS NIN**
*THE DIARY OF ANAÏS NIN, VOL. 1*

# STILLPOINTS: WHERE HEARTS
# AND MINDS MEET

*Stillpoints.* That's my word for moments in our lives when we are totally at one with the *now*; we are so *with* whatever we are doing or feeling or thinking that everything else seems to stop. There are no distractions from what we are experiencing or doing in that moment.

Stillpoints are moments when we entirely lose ourselves in what we're doing; there may be the sense that everything is unfolding on its own, even our own actions, like a flower blooming in an ultra-slow-motion film. Generally we feel calm and centered, having no need to even think about what we're doing. Everything, including our own thoughts, actions, and feelings, is happening with a wonderful effortlessness.

It might happen when you are walking in nature with a close friend, reading a book that totally engages you, listening to music, participating in an athletic event, while dancing, during sex — or with an infinite number of other experiences. Stillpoints are certainly akin to what the noted psychologist Abraham Maslow called *peak experiences*.

One of the qualities he identified was that after the experience we have a sense of being lucky, fortunate, or even "graced," of merging with the activity we were involved in.

In good writing, stillpoints are sometimes *aha!* moments, created when our words strike a special chord, expressing something clearly, authentically, and beautifully. Think of an experience or truth expressed as clearly as the ringing of a fine crystal bell.

Recall a stillpoint of your own and for a moment savor reliving that moment. You might want to start by just writing down images and feelings, maybe even thoughts associated with that moment. At first just take notes, as sketchy and personal as you wish. When you feel ready to do so, start crafting your notes into an article, poem, story, or vignette, whatever form the material itself wants to dictate. Flow with the writing, approaching it with playfulness and a sense of fun.

The closer you can come to describing anything as it really is, even the most gruesome and embarrassing, or uplifting, or unconscionable, or puzzling, or loving experience can become a stillpoint, reminding us of our own humanness. Stillpoints are those moments in all good writing that tell the truth so well that they seem like *déjà vu*, met with remarks such as, "Of course, I knew that!" Or, "That's so true!" None other than Margaret Thatcher said, "Of course it's the same old story. Truth usually is the same old story." The stillpoint is the writer's ability to tell the same old story so well that readers are able to clearly hear it for the first time.

*If you are a writer you locate yourself behind
a wall of silence and no matter what you
are doing, driving a car or walking or doing
housework...you can be writing, because
you have that space.*

— **JOYCE CAROL OATES**
IN *THE NEW YORKER*

# BUILDING MENTAL BRIDGES

When we're in the heat of writing, most of us focus our attention on getting the words down on paper, whether it's to communicate information to our readers, to tell a story, to entertain our readers, or to create a memorable poem. In your writing today, make a small shift in the way you think about your writing. Instead of focusing on the information you want to convey, think of yourself as *creating mental bridges* between your mind and your readers', that whatever you write is a vehicle for sharing the experience of your life with others.

Imagine that this complex and demanding language that we have developed over the millennia has evolved from a deep human need to exchange stories of our life experiences. We hunger to know how our inner lives are similar to others' as well as how they're unique. We want to believe that we are not alone in what we think and feel, and so we seek the intimacy and mutual understanding made possible through a shared language. We use language to dissolve our feelings of separateness, that is, to soften the sense of aloneness that philosophers and spiritual teachers say is central to human life.

The sophisticated use of language we share today

evolved from telling stories; storytellers were the original wisdom keepers and shamans. Through words they created the mythologies, the tales and fantasies that helped to explain what life is about. It is not so much that language captured the truth, or even that people necessarily believed the stories that were told, but it was a way of knowing what was going on in people's hearts and minds. It still does that today, though we all too easily forget that amid the glitter and dazzle of today's storytelling technologies — TV, the movies, and computer-generated special effects.

Thousands of years ago our ancestors told stories to help explain the mysteries of their lives — how the universe was created, the human tensions of love and hate, of peace and conflict, the inexplicable forces of the stars and moon, of birth and death. Our stories — whether fiction or nonfiction — explore the core questions of life and give us a way of seeing into other's lives.

Something unexpected occurs when we think of language not just as a way of recording or exchanging raw information but as creating an invisible bridge — a writer I know calls it a "spirit bridge" — between one consciousness and another. When viewed in this way, writer and reader touch mutual places in themselves that were perhaps invisible to them only moments before. Together we discover that the stories we tell ourselves and each other are, as Norman Fischer says in his book *Sailing Home*, "cover stories, narratives that hide within them deeper, underground narratives, that we can sense and taste now and again but never fully comprehend."

To understand language as a bridge between writers' and readers' consciousness is to acknowledge that whenever you write or speak you are entering a relationship. As with all relationships, there is an implied contract, not the least of which is to make certain you are heard and that you listen. It is not that your goal is to *please* your reader, any more than pleasing the other person is your only goal in your most intimate relationships. Psychologists are continually reminding us that we must be heard and seen in order for there to be a relationship; without that, there's essentially nobody there to have a relationship with! Nor can there be a relationship if one person dominates, speaking, giving orders, acting with no attention given to the other's wants and needs. For relationships to work, there's got to be a balance between listening and making yourself heard.

On the surface, it appears that as the author you are the dominant person in your relationship with your reader, for, after all, the book would not exist without you. But rest assured that readers are quite capable of chucking your book in the trash if they don't feel you are speaking to them — that somehow you have listened to them, have heard their wants and needs. In her book *Strength to Your Sword Arm*, author Brenda Ueland says:

> *Listening is a magnetic and strange thing, a creative force. You can see that when you think how the friends that really listen to us are the ones we move toward, and we want to sit in their radius as though it did us good, like ultraviolet rays.*

If you're like most of us who write, you will never meet in person more than a handful of your readers. So how can you listen? You listen even as you write, even as you put each word down on paper, just as a good speaker alternately absorbs and expresses ideas. For the writer, listening is not a passive act but something we do, an action. We do not hear just anyone, nor do we hear everyone, but knowing whom we hear and listening carefully make all the difference in the world. A modification of the saying "If you build it, they will come" helps to explain this process: "If you *listen*, they will come."

Take a few moments to describe the relationship you feel with your reader when you are most deeply immersed in your work; ask yourself how your reader is affected by what you have written. Who are you listening to when you write? What are their wants and needs? What makes them want to hear your stories and listen to what you have to say? Proceed with your writing knowing that you are never more generous than when you openly and humbly share your life experience with another.

*All your characters are you, virtuals of you;
writing is a controlled process of splitting into
virtual personalities in the safe haven of the page.
I can't tell you how to do that except to say that
it feels like self-hypnosis and probably is.
Controlled meditation helps. Once you've invented
a character and gotten to know her, you relax
into the role and she appears.*

## — RICHARD RHODES
*HOW TO WRITE*

# SEASIDE ADVENTURE

You are at a picturesque, perhaps even romantic, small seaside resort for a whole month. You've planned for this getaway for a long time, granting yourself this luxury in order to have uninterrupted time to write a book that you started three or four years before. You've been at it for three days and all is going well; just before dinner — which is served in the hotel dining room — you hear that a new guest has just arrived. You think nothing of it, but at dinner you look across the room and spot an old friend, eating alone at a table. He (or "she" — choose your gender) is apparently the guest who just arrived. Your eyes meet, there's a flash of recognition, and you cross to his table to greet him.

You are happy to see each other and decide to share a table since your dinners will soon be arriving. At first the conversation is very casual, mild chitchat, getting caught up and sharing minor details about your lives. Then your friend becomes serious and tells you about being in the midst of a bitter divorce.

The two of you finish your dinners and you ask your friend if he would like to talk further tonight. The answer is no — he offers some excuse — but you agree to meet for breakfast at 9 AM. The next morning, you go down to the

145

dining room and look around for your friend. After waiting for several minutes, you allow yourself to be seated. Nine o'clock passes, then nine thirty. You become concerned. You call his room and there's no answer. You order breakfast, finish eating, then go up to his room. You knock on the door but there's no answer. Since the door is slightly ajar, you push it open and step inside. Nobody is there, but there is luggage set down neatly by the door, monogrammed with your friend's initials. No personal items have been set out in the bathroom. Perhaps there is a paperback book on the bedside table. The bed is still neatly made and you guess that nobody slept in it the night before.

Pick up the story wherever you wish and tell where it goes from here. What has become of your friend? Does he suddenly return and find you standing there, having invaded his private space without permission? Could you (as well as your friend's luggage) be in the wrong room? Is your friend the victim of foul play? Are you told by the hostess that nobody was in that room last night, and there is no record of your friend ever having checked in? If so, how could this be? Is somebody lying? The mystery goes as deep as you wish to go with it.

*Once a human being has arrived on this earth, communication is the largest single factor determining what kinds of relationships he makes with others and what happens to him in the world about him.*

**— VIRGINIA SATIR**
*PEOPLEMAKING*

# PRETEND YOU'RE PSYCHIC
# (MAYBE YOU ARE!)

In the world of paranormal psychology, or PSI, there's a special technique known as *psychometry*. Those with this psychic gift hold an object in their hand and *tune in to* its history. For example, they might hold an antique wedding band, read its energy, and tell about the man or woman who wore it a hundred years ago. Similarly, there are psychics who find lost pets by reading the energy of a favorite chew toy, collar, or other object of the missing animal. And, of course, there are the psychic detectives hired by police departments to help locate missing persons or identify criminals by holding an object belonging to the victim or the perpetrator.

Without making a judgment one way or another about the validity of paranormal phenomena, prepare to have a little fun with it. Today you will make believe that you are a world-renowned psychic with extraordinary psychometric abilities.

Choosing an object to work with is the key. You'll probably have the most fun with an antique object that in some way fascinates you. The chances are good that you will be more enthralled by a beautiful antique fountain pen or a monogrammed lace hanky than you would by a coffee mug you bought at Starbuck's a few days before.

Once you've chosen your object, it's time to do a ritual to get you in the right frame of mind. Don't worry; it's just pretend. What might you do for this ritual? The answer is, whatever you think is appropriate. Sit down in a comfortable chair and light a candle. Place the object of your choice in front of you where you can easily touch it or pick it up and hold it in your hand. Close your eyes and create a mental picture of the object you are holding.

Now imagine that you are going back in time to the previous owners of this object. Ask yourself questions such as the following, and write down whatever answers come to mind:

- What were their names?

- How did the object come into their possession?

- In what ways did they use it?

- What were their feelings about it?

- What did the house or place of business where the object was usually kept look like?

- What human activities went on in the same location, which may or may not have involved the object?

- Was there someone who particularly prized the object? If so, what was that person like?

If it's a ring, necklace, or other personal item, describe the hand, neck, or whole body of the person who wore it.

After making some notes about what you discover from the exercise, make up a short vignette or story about the object. You might even include a characterization of the psychic — you — as she or he sat down to "read" the object. Who knows, you might just have the beginning of a short story, novel, or article.

Or the start of a career as a psychic!

# AWAKENING THE HUMAN SPIRIT

It is not just words that excite the creative writer and excite readers, but what those words evoke in the human spirit. In one respect, the power of language to stir the soul is a mystery as inexplicable as the glow we feel when we fall in love. How do we writers trigger such magic? How do we explain it? Surely, it's worth exploring. But to find it we need to bask in the mystery rather than analyzing these questions to death or even expecting to find a *solution*.

I'm reminded here of a story Barbara Kingsolver tells in a chapter titled "Postcards from the Imaginary Mom," from her book *High Tide in Tucson*. At the end of a long book tour, Kingsolver is asked by a television interviewer, "What is your book *about*?" She's tempted to answer, "It's *about* 300 pages long — *read it*!" Instead, after a long pause, and feeling like she is floundering, she answers, "It's not so much what happens... but how the words fit together, and what carries over from it into your own life."

Spend some time looking over passages from a book by your favorite author, in which it's *not so much what happens but how the words fit together, and what carries over from it into your own life*. What accomplishes this for you? How does your favorite writer put sentences together in such a way that something is carried from his or her life into yours? What kinds of imagery does he or she use to move you in this way? Is there a particular rhythm to her or his language? Is there a distinct tone or attitude expressed? Does the author use sensory language, that is, words describing sensations such as color, sound, taste, touch? How personally involved does the author seem to be in what she or he is saying? Do you feel the author's emotional involvement and identify with it?

Moments ago, my eyes turned to a book on the tall shelf to the left of my desk. I spotted the spine of a collection of stories by Norman Maclean and reached out for it. The lead story of the collection is *A River Runs Through It*, made popular in the 1990s by a Robert Redford film starring Brad Pitt. It wasn't the film I remembered so much as a passage from the book that I'd marked with what was now a faded yellow highlight. Toward the end of the story, the narrator's father asks him about his writing, and the narrator explains that he likes to tell stories that are true. The father suggests that after he's finished writing stories that are true, maybe his son should make up a story and all the people to go in it. He tells his son, "Only then will you understand what happened and why."

And then the author, Maclean, who was seventy when he wrote this, says, "Now nearly all those I loved and did not understand when I was young are dead, but I still reach out to them."

For me this is a deeply poignant moment in the story,

for it touches upon a truism not just for writers but for all of us, about the importance of friendship and love, and how elusive is our knowledge of ourselves and others. As a writer I'm reminded that we usually get to the truth through our own fictions, that is, by *making up* the story and the people who go in it. And I might add that whether we're writing fiction, nonfiction, memoir, or poetry, whatever we get down on paper, no matter how true it might be, is still make-believe, our own creations of whatever truths we perceive. The important thing is, does our way of telling our stories, the way we put the sentences together, move the human spirit?

When you're looking for exemplary writings from your favorite authors, I recommend that instead of going to the masters — Dickens, Hemingway, Shakespeare, Tolstoy, Hellman, Kingsolver, Walker, or any of the usual suspects — you choose ones you don't worship. Look at the work of authors who seem more accessible to you, perhaps ones who are your contemporaries. Why? Because, if you're at all like me, you'll compare your own writing to that of one of the greats who's been placed on a pedestal by generations before us and you'll *just know* that attaining such heights would be like climbing Mount Everest. When you're tempted to compare yourself to others, don't. Instead, remember that you are like no other being who has ever walked the planet. Creativity has much to do with recognizing this truth and embracing how you are different, not by measuring yourself against what others have done.

When you find a passage that you feel awakens the human spirit, that strongly carries over from the writing into your own life, copy it — yes, I do mean *copy*, word for word. I don't mean pass it off as your own work. (Remember, you are like no other.) But copying another's writings while being attentive to how it feels to put the sentences down on paper, just as the other author once did, can help you get inside that writer's mind, understanding her or his creative process. Try this with several different writers and notice the differences you experience between one author and another, how their words go together in a particular way, and what they do to achieve the emotional and perhaps spiritual effects they do. Notice that I didn't say to compare one author to another but to notice their differences without ranking them.

Don't worry that you will lose your own unique voice as you do this copying exercise. If anything, it will allow you to recognize and honor the differences between one writer and another, and that includes recognizing and honoring differences between you and them. Knowing how we're different and welcoming the diverse paths we all forge to arrive at the same destination — the awakening of the human spirit — frees you to discover your own voice.

*The aesthetic view of life is not confined to those who can create or appreciate works of art. It exists wherever natural senses play freely on the manifold phenomena of our world, and when life as a consequence is found to be full of felicity.*

— **HERBERT READ**

*ANNALS OF INNOCENCE*
*AND EXPERIENCE*

# THE LOST DIAMOND SOLITAIRE

This is a story about Joanna, who has fallen on difficult times and is financially bereft. You can elaborate on her problems as much as you wish. Maybe she's broken up with her lover or a spouse. Maybe there's been a tragedy in her family. Perhaps she's lost a job or she's recently discovered a health challenge that she must confront.

To cheer her up, her friend takes her to the opera, which is something Joanna loves to do. At intermission, there's a long line for the bathroom. Instead of getting in line, Joanna waits till the opera begins again, then returns to the bathroom, where she finds herself alone.

She is washing her hands when she looks down and notices something sparkling in the trap in the sink. She sees that it is a ring and realizes that by using tweezers that she just happens to have in her purse, she can retrieve it. After several tries, she finally rescues the ring from the drain trap. At first she thinks it must surely be mere costume jewelry, of little or no value. But as she rinses it off she realizes that it is much more. She holds in her fingers a large diamond solitaire, at least a carat and a half. Having once worked in a jewelry store, she recognizes its considerable value.

She excitedly slips it into her purse. She knows that this ring could be the answer to all her financial woes. She is still drying her hands when a very distressed young woman, expensively dressed, bursts into the room. Nearly hysterical, she asks Joanna if she has seen a ring that must have slipped from her finger while she was washing her hands. Her fiancé had given it to her only the evening before and she had not yet had it sized.

Joanna is filled with conflict. She has little doubt that the ring she found belongs to this young woman. But what proof does she have? One doesn't just hand over such a valuable object on hearsay alone. Besides, judging by what she is wearing, including her other jewelry, the woman is obviously very wealthy. What does she know of the grief and hardship Joanna is suffering? The woman could easily replace this lost ring.

Finish the story, telling about Joanna's inner conflicts and what she ultimately decides to do about the ring.

# WHAT GOES AROUND...

The main character for this story is a woman. I'll call her Dawn, but feel free to rename her as you write her story in the third person. Here's the premise: Dawn moved to this town three years ago to recover from a difficult divorce. She is only now looking for ways to expand her circle of friends. One day a neighbor invites her to get together with a reading group she is starting. Dawn, who is an avid reader, jumps at the opportunity. This will be a chance to meet people with common interests — or who at least are readers.

On the night of the first meeting, at least a half-dozen people show up. The hostess has everyone form a circle in her living room. After people have settled down a bit, she asks her guests to go around the circle and introduce themselves. Each person in turn is instructed to tell a little about her personal life and briefly describe the most recent book she's read.

Everything goes well until it comes to a woman sitting directly across from Dawn. While Simone is obviously making an effort to be as unemotional as possible, it soon becomes clear to everyone that she is in great distress. Sobbing, she reveals that she is going through a bitter divorce from her husband of eight years. As her story unfolds Dawn realizes, to her horror, that Simone is the "other woman" who caused Dawn's separation and divorce just three years before. Dawn is shocked and many emotions are stirred up. But before Simone has completed her story, Dawn feels a major change taking place inside herself.

Every woman in the circle introduces herself and tells her own story. Dawn barely hears what any of them say. She only remembers Simone's story and how that woman's story is affecting her. After the meeting, Dawn goes up to Simone and asks if she would be willing to join her for a drink. Simone agrees and half an hour later they are sitting together at a small table in a quiet neighborhood bar.

Now it's your turn. Describe this meeting in the bar. What do Dawn and Simone discuss? What is the change that came over Dawn as she listened to Simone's story at their mutual friend's home? This is a great opportunity for writing lively dialogue and exploring classic literary themes such as jealousy, rage, bewilderment, courage, forgiveness, compassion, and even the roots of friendship.

# TALK TO YOUR READERS

One of the secrets of truly engaging writing, whether fiction or nonfiction, is the author's ability to make her readers feel she is really speaking to them. Rarely is this secret of good writing taught in school or even in creative writing classes, yet it is a powerful ingredient in most successful books — with the possible exception of some technical manuals. Creating this sense of intimacy with your reader is a skill that is easy to learn. When you write in this way, not only will you connect with your readers, but writing itself will become more exciting for you. So how is this to be accomplished?

The trick is to use your imagination to create an "ideal reader" in your mind. To jumpstart this process, think of what happens when you write a letter to a close friend or family member. If you're like me, you quickly start imagining how your friend will be affected by what you are saying. Will she be happy to learn that you have taken a job in a city twenty miles from where she lives? How will your friend react if you tell her that you don't like her fiancé? When you imagine the responses of the person you're writing to, that person comes alive in your mind. And therein lies the secret of this process. When the reader comes alive in your mind, your writing becomes more lively and engaging. You take your reader into your confidence with every word you put down on paper. The end result is that your readers will experience a sense of connection with you, similar to what you experience when you are writing; you convey to your readers that you were thinking of them and taking their lives into consideration.

Take your time to create this ideal reader in your mind with every article, story, or book that you write. Every now and then pause and ask yourself questions such as, "How will she take this?" Or, "Am I explaining this point in a way he or she can easily comprehend?" The more time you take to remember your reader in this way, the more powerful and intimate your writing will become, reaching into your readers' lives and letting them reach into yours. Your readers will be deeply engaged, and they'll think you're magic with your ability to "know" their minds and feelings.

Write a short profile of your ideal reader, perhaps someone you know, or maybe a character you've created, whom you imagine to be deeply interested in your writing. Include at least a few lines of dialogue in which she tells you what it is about your writing that captures her interest.

*You may write for the joy of it, but the act of writing is not complete in itself. It has its end in its audience.*

— **FLANNERY O'CONNOR**
IN *THE HABIT OF BEING,*
EDITED BY SALLY FITZGERALD

# IT WAS A DARK
# AND STORMY NIGHT

If I were given to hyperbole, which I can assure you I *never am*, I'd be tempted to repeat what thousands of other writing coaches have said before me: that the opening paragraph is the most important part of anything you write. There's certainly some truth in this. Obviously, if you don't hook your readers on the first page — and preferably within the first three sentences — they may not read the rest. This is particularly true of readers such as literary agents and acquisitions editors who have stacks of manuscripts to read every day. Their vetting process begins with the first words they read from your manuscript, and if you don't catch their attention right away, it's as good an excuse as any to stuff your pages into your SASE, jam in a standard rejection form, and toss it in the outbasket heading for the post office.

The most famous — or perhaps infamous — opening lines are those penned in 1830 by Edward George Bulwer-Lytton:

> *It was a dark and stormy night; the rain fell in torrents except at occasional intervals, when it was*

*checked by a violent gust of wind which swept up*
*the streets (for it is in London that our scene lies),*
*rattling along the housetops, and fiercely agitating*
*the scanty flame of the lamps that struggled against*
*the darkness.*

In 1982, Professor Scott Rice of the English department at San Jose State University was prompted by these lines and similarly florid openers by his students to sponsor the Bulwer-Lytton Fiction Contest, a "whimsical literary competition" of opening sentences for the worst possible novels. And, yes, the contest is still open. Learn the rules for submission at www.bulwer-lytton.com. Or send your own entry to:

Bulwer-Lytton Fiction Contest
Department of English
San Jose State University
San Jose, CA 95192-0090

All kidding aside, opening lines can make or break a perfectly good or even brilliant piece of writing, whether it's a short, nonfiction magazine article or a multigenerational historical novel of a thousand pages. Opening lines are particularly important today, because authors are competing with TV and movies in which camera techniques, sex, violence, and big bangs grab our attention by stimulating the most basic fears and desires of the reptilian brain.

The most effective opening lines accomplish two things: they grab the reader's attention (the hook), and they focus on either the protagonist's dilemma, if it's a work of fiction, or the subject area you're going to explore, if it's a nonfiction work. Remember that most readers will have a thousand different things on their minds when they come upon your writing, and it will only be after you have their attention that you'll even show up on their radar. Never underestimate the skill it requires to get their attention and focus it. (An author friend of mine advised me that to accomplish this you need the verbal equivalent of what you use to get a donkey's attention — a sturdy 2 x 4 about four feet long.)

In a nonfiction book titled *Connections: The Five Threads of Intuitive Wisdom*, Gabrielle Roth wrote:

> *At fifteen, I jumped into the back seat of a friend's car, ready to take off on an excellent adventure with five of my friends. Suddenly my mother came flying across our front lawn waving a wooden spoon covered in chocolate icing, yelling, "Gabrielle, get out of that car. You can't go!"*

Before the end of that first page, we learn that two blocks from her home another car ran a stoplight and demolished the back of the car where Gabrielle would have been sitting. This lesson in trusting your intuition — or at least your mother's — hooks us and brings us immediately into the author's world.

Here's the opening line from *The Miracle Life of Edgar Mint*, a novel by Brady Udall, about a half-Apache

165

child growing up in the dysfunctional world of foster homes in the American West:

> *If I could tell you only one thing about my life it would be this: when I was seven years old the mailman ran over my head. As formative events go, nothing else comes close.*

In a mere thirty-five words the author has captured our attention, focused it on the protagonist, and given us a very powerful clue that this is going to be a book about great adversity — one hopes being overcome.

With these principles in mind — hooking your readers and focusing their attention — think about something you have written or that you have in progress. Write an opening paragraph that does what those examples do for the readers.

# WRITER'S BLOCK? TELL YOUR READER ABOUT IT

Do you dread *writer's block* as much as most of us do? You pick up your pen or turn on your computer, and nothing springs to mind. No words. No images. No story. Nothing! Your muse has flown the coop. You start a few lines, get a couple paragraphs down on paper, but none of it goes anywhere. Dead ends! Your mind is as blank as the computer screen or that glaringly white sheet of paper waiting for your scratchings. After an agonizing hour of gazing into the void, you plunge into gloom. You're convinced your creative juices have dried up. Your worst fears bubble to the surface . . . and you brood . . . surely this is final proof that you were never cut out to be a writer!

Your inner critics begin chanting their mind-numbing mantras: What ever made you think anyone would be interested in anything you have to say? What made you believe you had a gift for words? Why don't you try doing something useful with your life?

Though I've suffered through dry spells myself, I've never found that these dark whispers from my inner critics signaled the end of my creative life. Rather, they are nearly always traced to a rather unexpected source — losing touch with my readers, or not being in touch with them at the moment I sat down to write.

Ralph Waldo Emerson said, "'Tiz the good reader that makes the good book." There's more than a grain of truth in this. If your reader isn't an active participant in your creative process, you're just talking to yourself, and that's the crux of the problem. If you are only talking to yourself, or readers just like you, the readers you're imagining already know what you have to say. What reason do they have to listen to you? Remember the last time someone tried to tell you a story you'd already heard a few times before? You probably weren't the best listener, nor would your lack of interest have fed the storyteller's eagerness to go on. Here's a secret your English teacher probably didn't tell you: *You do your best writing when you're imagining your words reaching an interested reader, preferably one who hangs on your every word.*

I believe we all sense when we're not connecting with our readers or when we're only talking to ourselves. Not so coincidentally, that's often when our inner critics start nagging us: *What makes you think anyone would be interested in what you have to say?* You may think that inner critic is putting you down. But maybe not. Maybe that question is a more constructive one, asking you, in all seriousness, if you really understand what might interest your reader. What do you in fact have to offer?

Whether you've got writer's block or are just feeling lackadaisical about your writing, the cure I offer is quite simple: Find out more about the reader you have in mind. Write a letter to them! Don't worry, this is an imaginary letter. You are not going to send it to anyone. The letter could be to a real person or to a character you create. Imagine this reader will love hearing from you and will be receptive to what you write. They don't know as much as you do about the subject you're covering. They haven't heard the stories you have to tell.

Tell your imaginary reader in this letter what's going on in your mind at this moment — the truth of this moment, whatever it might be. Tell them what it's like to have writer's block. Tell them what you want to impart in your writing. Tell them what you'd like readers to get from your creative efforts. If you are writing fiction, talk about characters you have in mind, what you like about them and any difficulty you're having as you develop them.

How far should you take this? As far as you want. I know several writers who do this exercise for their daily journal work or whenever they feel stuck. These letters bring your readers alive in your creative consciousness, forming the boundless circle between author and reader that gives all successful writing its spark. Do this exercise regularly and you'll get some wonderful creative surprises!

# CABIN IN THE WOODS

With his writing of *Walden Pond* in the mid-1800s, Henry David Thoreau established himself as an American icon that is as alive today as it was a century and a half ago. While that author's back-to-the-land experience lasted for just a bit more than two years, he articulated the dream of self-reliance and renewing our bond with nature. The themes of getting away from it all, of returning to nature and proving that we have the inner resources to get along on our own, are echoed throughout our literature and our social movements. We see them in everything from writings by Thoreau's contemporary Henry Wadsworth Longfellow, whose poetry romanticized the "noble savage," to William Faulkner's 1946 novella *The Bear*, to the back-to-the-land movement of the 1960s and 1970s to escape the problems of city life and rediscover the laws of nature, to Werner Herzog's film *Grizzly Man* (2005), documenting Timothy Treadwell's ultimately disastrous effort to prove his compatibility with grizzly bears in the Alaskan wilderness.

Going to the wilderness calls upon us to sort out what's truly necessary and to presumably "simplify" our lives by getting more in touch with the earth. An acquaintance of mine led wilderness camps for a living, taking people on river trips and into survival adventures, as he called them, where for several days they got along on little more than their own wits. He once remarked that these activities gave people an opportunity to escape from their "storage locker" thinking, a reference to accumulating such masses of material goods that we have to rent secure spaces away from our homes to keep them.

What are some of the lessons and insights that our own Walden Pond adventures might offer? Here's an opportunity to find out without ever leaving your home. Okay, it might not be exactly like actually trekking off into the wilderness with nothing but a backpack and a bottle of water, but it's a start.

Imagine that you have rented a cabin described in an ad on Craigslist or your favorite social networking site. All you have to go on is the following:

> *Getaway Cabin Available. Fireplace but no utilities. Small, sound, and nicely sited in pine forest. Lake with fish and spring a short hike away. Moderate hike from road 231. Will supply map.*

After talking briefly with the owner, you send some money and receive a single photo and a roughly drawn map of the area.

*The assignment:* Write about your adventures at the cabin, where you stayed for two weeks. Here are some ideas to work with:

- What equipment and supplies did you pack in?

- Did you have any trouble finding the path to the cabin?

- Describe any problems you encountered on your way to the cabin.

- Describe your first impressions upon arriving at the cabin.

- Was there wildlife in the vicinity? How did animals relate to you?

- Did you find the trail to the lake and spring easy or difficult?

- Describe the lake and spring as you first found it.

- How did you cook?

- What did you eat?

- How did you deal with garbage and human waste?

- How was your first night there?

- Did you have any unexpected visitors?

- Describe any challenges you had around the weather.

- What new understandings did you have about your relationship with nature?

- Did you create anything to make your life in the wilderness more comfortable?

- What happened that you hadn't anticipated, and what did you do about it?

Finish this exercise by reflecting on any insights you might have had during this experience that revealed something to you about your everyday life at home.

# SENSORY INTELLIGENCE

Any time you wish to bring your reader into a scene in the story, embellish your writing with adjectives describing the senses — sounds, scents, tastes, physical touch, and images. Examples: the *red* wheelbarrow, the *velvety* skin of the dog's nose, the *bitter* lemon, the *booming* vibrations of the kettle drum, the chill winter breeze on the child's *tender* cheeks.

Here's a writing exercise to stretch your imagination. Choose one or more of the following to write about:

- Describe a bird in flight, focusing only on physical sensations that you would feel if you were flying.

- Describe a luxurious banquet from the point of view of a waiter who is prevented from tasting the food; describe the scene only through sight, sound, touch, and smell.

- Describe a concert from a deaf person's point of view, telling only what you see and what you physically feel.

- Describe a joyous experience using only words about sensations — what you see, hear, smell, taste, and touch. Use no emotional, spiritual, or intellectual descriptors.

*The material of your life is yours to claim and use. It's also yours to bend, stretch, mold, and change. Part of finding your voice is giving yourself permission to use your life and the lives around you for material — and then to distort that material outrageously. Events of your life can be a starting point. But you need to give your voice permission and range to draw on other events and lives as well as your own imagination.*

**— THAISA FRANK AND DOROTHY WALL**
*FINDING YOUR WRITER'S VOICE*

# RAW MATERIAL OF THE
# WRITER'S CRAFT

The writer of poetry, fiction, or nonfiction treats the inner life, whether painful or blissful, as the raw material of the craft, just as the potter treats the clay, or the carpenter a pile of lumber, or a cook the foods and herbs he or she uses as the raw material of art. While we need to heal our inner wounds so that they don't cripple or paralyze us, we also need to realize that without their imagery and tensions we'd have little to draw from for our creative life. We'd be like the potter with no clay or the carpenter with no nails or wood or the cook with no food or fire.

Look upon everything from your inner world as being material just waiting to be transformed through your craft. Think about the imagery from your childhood that still affects you when you see it or read about it — the countryside or the cityscape around you, a favorite toy you once had, the face of a loved one, an activity you enjoyed, a favorite food, a place you visited with your family, a scene where you were particularly happy or frightened, or where you felt cared for and loved. Write a few paragraphs describing a scene — either fictional or true — that uses this imagery from your past or that is built around an incident that occurred. Remember, it's okay to fictionalize any of the raw material that comes up from your past.

# THE OLD BOOKSTORE

You are browsing through the stacks in an old used bookstore. While you are in your favorite aisle of the store, a single book falls from the shelf and nearly hits you on the head. You pick it up off the floor. It is an ancient, wellworn leather-bound copy. As you examine the title page you are startled to see that the author's name is the same as yours but this book was published fifty years before you were born. Bursting with curiosity, you purchase the book, rush home with it, and spend the next several hours reading it. As you go through the book, you may come upon some extra surprises, such as an inscription, paragraphs that are underlined, marginal notes, or even a letter, newspaper clipping, or lock of hair all but hidden between the pages. Tell what you discover about the book, and about yourself, as a result of finding and reading this book.

*Where the storyteller is loyal, eternally and unswervingly loyal to the story, there, in the end, silence will speak. Where the story has been betrayed, silence is but emptiness.*

**— ISAK DINESEN**
"THE BLANK PAGE," IN *LAST TALES*

# VARIATION IS
# THE SPICE OF WRITE

We all tend to develop habits in our writing, as in everything else in our lives. This is not necessarily a bad thing. We find something that works well for us, then perhaps refine it a bit, and thereafter we stick to doing it that way over and over again, for the sake of efficiency, accuracy, and predictability. Up to a point, this works fine. The downside is that, if the repetition is in the way we write, we stop paying close attention to what we're doing. We fall back on the routine, repeating the ways of working that we've come to depend on. Pretty soon we're getting lazy and — God forbid — we're letting ourselves slip in a cliché now and then. We are soon writing on automatic pilot. Our brains begin to doze. And be assured, if the writer is dozing the reader will be too.

The truth is, your brain loves variation and change; think of them as super-food for your all-important cerebral cortex. Brain researchers over the past decade or two have spent a great deal of time on neuroplasticity, that is, our brains' ability to renew themselves regardless of age. Scientists have shown that the healthy human brain can form billions of new connections and patterns, over and over again, even into the latter years of our lives. I'm simplifying a bit here, but what the scientists tell us about *neuroplasticity* is that when we set out to learn something new, or when we vary the way we do a routine or habit we've already developed, millions, and sometimes billions, of new connections — synapses — can occur. In the process we grow millions upon millions of new brain cells. And all of this is super-food for our creativity.

Any time we write a poem or story, make a new journal entry, or start writing a new book, our brains are literally afire with activity. If we could take a photo of all the synaptic charges at such times it would look like the most extravagant Fourth of July fireworks display. What's more, the new connections don't go away. Our brains continue to make and use whatever new connections, patterns, and neurons are formed.

It's my belief that one of the great side benefits of rewriting your own work is that it offers an opportunity to work with these principles of neuroplasticity, if you're willing to take some chances and not cling to what you've already written. By introducing something new and different into writing you've already done — and which you thought you'd finished — your brain has to do a lot of new juggling. Plus, your changes usually make the writing more interesting and clearer for your readers.

Here's a demonstration, using three lines from a novel of mine (*Spirit Circle*) published several years ago:

The original: *A huge bolt of lightning ripped across the sky to the south, and like a gigantic Preying Mantis it appeared to squat momentarily over the earth. Instantly, the skies opened up and the rain poured down, splattering gigantic drops off the hood of the Jeep as it headed back downhill.*

I set myself the goal — quite arbitrarily — of reversing the order of the action, so that the scene would begin with the movement of the Jeep instead of ending with it. I would then enhance my description of the storm so that it would be more atmospheric and ominous than the original. Here's the outcome.

The rewrite: *As she turned the Jeep and headed downhill, the leaden sky to the south suddenly opened up, filling with light. A thunderbolt, miles long, sprouted four shining limbs. Hovering in the sky like a giant Preying Mantis, it danced across the silhouetted mountaintops. Thunder rumbled and the luminous creature vanished, plunging the earth into darkness.*

I recommend randomly picking a paragraph that you've written during the past few months and doing some major rewrites. This doesn't mean you have to use the rewrite in the original piece. Maybe you'll want to keep what you had. The point here is to give your brain a creative workout.

Randomly select a paragraph from your own writing, fiction, nonfiction, or poetry. Copy and paste so that you have a separate copy of what you're going to rewrite. Since the original is still safely in place, you are free of any resistance you might have to changing the original.

Start with simply changing the order of sentences in the paragraph. Or introduce new colors. Or decide that you are going to reduce the number of sentences you use. Or maybe, as I did, you will try to capture a whole different mood or quality. Then let your brain play with this rewrite. Look for elements to introduce that don't at first feel comfortable or familiar. Open a dictionary or other book to a random page and blindly put your finger on a single word or portion of a sentence. Try integrating that word, or words, into your rewrite, just to see what happens.

The point of this exercise is not just to rewrite the scene so that it's *better* — smoother, free of errors, clearer — but to set yourself goals for rewriting that will encourage your brain to reach deeper and reinvent what's already on the page.

Pay particular attention to the subtle tensions of your mind as you do this exercise. Notice any creative bursts along the way, moments when you get a sudden insight or see a new way of phrasing something. Realize that every time you create something new on the page, your brain is forming new patterns and even growing new neurons. This is creativity expanding, refining, becoming richer and more adept.

# KNOW WHEN
# ENOUGH IS ENOUGH

Always remember that writing is an alliance between author and reader. With every line we put down on the page, we need to leave room for the reader's imagination and intellect. Too much information and the reader's participation is squeezed out; too little and they're adrift. So, how do we judge when enough is enough — not too little and not too much? It's easy to see the problem in live conversations, especially the kind we get into at parties and social gatherings lubricated by a too-generous flow of alcohol. You know the situation. You get cornered by someone, more than a little tipsy, who is talking so loud and fast you can't get a word in edgewise. Frustrating to say the least! Your discomfort escalates while you search for an escape route. At the opposite extreme are those moments when you find yourself with a casual acquaintance who is so reticent you're having to hold up both ends of the conversation.

It's not just what the other person is saying or not saying that's the problem. Rather, it's that their participation or lack of it leaves you feeling disappointed or discounted because your presence and your needs are obviously not very important to the speaker or writer. Maybe they're using you as a sounding board for their ideas. Or they are trying to impress you. Or they're intimidated. Or maybe they're trying to establish themselves as alpha dog, a verbal form of marking the territory. And sometimes it's just that they have low self-esteem, are shy, or want to be invisible.

The bottom line is that they aren't looking for much interaction with you. The same dynamics may be at work on the printed page, with the writer saying either too little or too much. In most cases, it's the latter. The following excerpt came in the middle of the writer's story about the reconciliation of two friends. This scene was in the story to illustrate the tension between the two characters as Sharon made this peacemaking overture to her friend Miriam:

*Sharon walked into Miriam's cramped little office where her friend was still hard at work on her PC. Miriam's desk was set up so that anyone sitting at it would be facing the blank white wall that was peppered with pinholes and bits of yellowed tape where people had fastened things in the past. There were stacks of messy papers everywhere, including on the floor, an ancient orange and black shag rug dating back to the '50s that probably hadn't even been vacuumed in years. Miriam wore faded blue jeans and a rumpled grey sweatshirt with the name of a college emblazoned across the chest. Miriam herself looked as if she'd been sleeping in those same clothes for several days. Bent over the keyboard, she was clacking away and staring at the screen without looking up to acknowledge her friend as she entered.*

*"Hello," Sharon said, standing in the doorway feeling anxious and uneasy, like an intruder in her friend's little domain.*

*"Hi, Sharon," Miriam answered, mechanically, confirming what Sharon was feeling about being an intruder in this space. "How're you doing?"*

*"I'm okay," Sharon replied. "How about you?"*

*"I'm good," Miriam said, her voice like a robot on automatic pilot. It wasn't difficult to determine that she was pretending to be friendly but she really was nervous about Sharon being in the room at all. Miriam didn't even glance away from the computer screen, which danced with squiggles that became the words she was typing. All of this totally confirmed Sharon's feelings that maybe she shouldn't have even bothered to come here.*

*"What are you working on?" Sharon asked, even though she was feeling uncomfortable. Not that it was any great mystery why there was so much tension in the room. There was a good reason that Miriam was being so withdrawn and uncommunicative.*

When the author read this scene to the writing class, nearly everyone thought the piece was overwritten. She used way too many words to show the tension between these two characters. They suggested that she cut the scene way down and do less "telling" and more "showing." Here's that author's rewrite:

*As Sharon opened the door to Miriam's cramped little office her friend was clacking away on the keyboard of her PC. All around her were stacks of paper. Crumpled scraps spilled onto the floor from the overfull wastebasket. Miriam looked like she'd been sleeping in the same jeans and sweatshirt for several days.*

*"Hi," Sharon said, standing stiffly just inside the door.*

*Miriam mumbled a curt greeting but didn't look up. "What can I do for you?"*

*Sharon stepped forward and planted herself next to the desk, forcing Miriam to look up, then said, "We need to talk. And now!"*

The rewrite was truly lean and mean — from three hundred words down to one hundred. Yet everyone agreed that the author got her point across perfectly, giving readers just the right amount of information to bring the scene alive in their own imaginations. The author's classmates said there was more tension created in the shorter version than in the longer one because as readers they weren't being told what to feel.

Lean and mean detail isn't always desired. Sometimes you really want to immerse your reader in physical details to reflect a character's frame of mind. In an interview in *Writer's Digest*, author Stephen King made the point that "reader absorption comes in the details: An overturned tricycle in the gutter of an abandoned neighborhood can stand for everything."

The following is my rewrite inspired by my student writer's scene, using additional details, such as the messiness of the office and the blanket balled up in the corner, to suggest Miriam's deterioration and a possible slide toward a mental breakdown. While this departs from the writer's original intent, my hope is that it illustrates how you can use details to tell about more than the room:

*Sharon tapped lightly on the door, then eased into Miriam's cramped little office where her friend was hunkered over her PC. Miriam's desk faced the dingy blank wall, once painted white but now smudged with fingerprints and scarred with nail holes and tabs of used tape that once held notes or clippings. Untidy stacks of paper spilled across the desk, with several file folders trailing their contents out onto the floor. Sharon wondered how long it had been since the aging orange and black shag rug had been vacuumed. Probably months.*

*Miriam wore faded blue jeans and a rumpled grey sweatshirt with "University of Hard Blocks" emblazoned across the back. The wearer herself looked as if she'd lived in those same clothes for several days. Her hair was tangled and dull. Judging from the blanket balled up in the corner, she hadn't left this room even to sleep.*

*Bent over the keyboard, Miriam continued to clack away, staring trancelike into the computer screen.*

*"Miriam," Sharon said. "Tell me what's going on here."*

*"I'm good. Don't worry about me. Working. You can see that...." Miriam's voice trailed off, robotic and cold, like noises spilling from a machine, barely approximating human speech.*

*Sharon crossed the room and planted herself at the left side of the desk, forcing Miriam to look up, then said, "I want you to stop, Miriam. Right now. I want you to take your eyes off the computer and look at me. We need to talk. Now!"*

It's difficult to generalize about how much is enough or how much is too much. Sometimes the details strengthen what you're writing; sometimes they simply distract, all but eliminating the reader's contribution to the creative process. As has often been said, god is in the details — or was it the devil?

Maybe all we have to do is ask ourselves, "How can I best achieve what Stephen King describes as reader absorption?"

Enough said?

# Works Referenced

Barbara Abercrombie. *Courage and Craft: Writing Your Life Story*. New World Library, 2007.

Marilee Adams. *Change Your Questions, Change Your Life*. Berrett-Koehler, 2004, 2009.

Lynn V. Andrews. *Medicine Woman,* 25th anniversary edition. Tarcher, 2006.

Simone de Beauvoir. *Force of Circumstance.* Da Capo, 1994.

William Blake. *Jerusalem: The Emanation of the Giant Albion*. Kessinger, 2004

Margaret Bourke-White. *Portrait of Myself*. G. K. Hall, 1985.

Catherine Drinker Bowen. In *The Atlantic,* 1957.

Rita Mae Brown. *Starting from Scratch*. Bantam, 1989.

Orson Scott Card. *Characters and Viewpoint*. Writer's Digest Books, 1999.

Joan Didion. *The Writer and Her Work*, ed. Janet Sternburg. W. W. Norton, 2000.

Isak Dinesen. *Last Tales*. Random House, 1957.

Jim Dodge. *Fup*. Simon & Schuster, 1983.

Oriah Mountain Dreamer. *The Invitation*. Harper One, 1999.

Leif Enger. *Peace Like a River*. Atlantic Monthly Press, 2002.

Norman Fischer. *Sailing Home*. Free Press, 2008.

Gustave Flaubert. *The Letters of Gustave Flaubert*. Harvard University Press, 1982.

Thaisa Frank and Dorothy Wall. *Finding Your Writer's Voice*. St Martin's, 1994.

Philip Furia. "As Time Goes By: Creating Biography." In *Writing Creative Nonfiction*, ed. Carolyn Forché and Philip Gerard. Writers Digest Books, 2001.

Indira Gandhi. In *Speeches and Writings*. Harper & Row, 1975.

Ernest Hemingway. *Death in the Afternoon*. Scribner, 1960.

Napoleon Hill. *Think and Grow Rich*. Aventine Press, 2004.

C.G. Jung. *Memories, Dreams, Reflections*. Vintage, 1963.

———. *Psychological Types*. Princeton University Press, 1976.

Franz Kafka. *The Metamorphosis*. Hodder and Stoughton, 1999.

Stephen King and Jerry B. Jenkins. "The WD Interview," by Jessica Strawser. *Writer's Digest*, May/June 2009.

Barbara Kingsolver. *High Tide in Tucson*. HarperCollins, 1995.

———. *Small Wonder*. Harper Perennial, 2003.

Anne Lamott. *Bird by Bird: Some Instructions on Writing and Life*. Anchor, 1995.

Ursula K. Le Guin. *The Earthsea Trilogy*. Houghton Mifflin, 2005.

———. "Prophets and Mirrors." In *The Living Light*, fall 1970, 111–21.

Barry Holstun Lopez. *River Notes: The Dance of Herons*. Avon Books, 1980.

Norman Maclean. *A River Runs Through It and Other Stories*. University of Chicago Press, 1976.

Don Marquis. "Mehitabel Was Once Cleopatra." In *The Annotated Archy and Mehitabel*. Penguin Classics, 2006.

Abraham H. Maslow. *The Farther Reaches of Human Nature*. Penguin, 1993.

Henry Miller. *Henry Miller on Writing*. New Directions, 1964.

Anaïs Nin. *The Diary of Anaïs Nin*. Harvest Books, 1969.

Joyce Carol Oates. In *The New Yorker*. June 1963.

Flannery O'Connor. *The Habit of Being: The Letters of Flannery O'Connor*, ed. Sally Fitzgerald. Farrar, Straus and Giroux, 1988.

Herbert Read. *Annals of Innocence and Experience*. Haskell House, 1974.

Richard Rhodes. *How to Write: Advice and Reflections.* Harper, 1996.

Gabrielle Roth. *Connections: The Five Threads of Intuitive Wisdom.* Tarcher, 2004.

May Sarton. *Crucial Conversations: Tools for Talking When the Stakes Are High.* McGraw Hill, 2002.

Virginia Satir. *The New Peoplemaking.* Science and Behavior Books, 1988.

Evelyn Scott. *Escapade.* Carroll & Graf, 1987.

Ilana Simons. *A Life of One's Own: A Guide to Better Living Through the Work and Wisdom of Virginia Woolf.* Penguin, 2007.

John Steinbeck. "Johnny Bear," in *The Portable Steinbeck.* Penguin, 1976.

Margaret Thatcher. In *Time.* 1981.

Mark Twain. *The Adventures of Huckleberry Finn.* Bantam Classics, 1981.

Brady Udall. *The Miracle Life of Edgar Mint.* Vintage, 2002.

Brenda Ueland. *Strength to Your Sword Arm.* Holy Cow! Press, 1996.

Alice Walker. *The Color Purple.* Harvest Books, 2006.

# Going Further: An Annotated Bibliography

These are books from my own shelves. They're authors I've enjoyed reading and learning from. I have listed them here alphabetically to avoid being accused of playing favorites — or, more precisely, to dodge the impossible task of rating which ones I like best. (You'll probably be able to tell that from what I say anyway.) The short paragraphs I've written are not intended to give the whole story of what each book offers. My goal was much more modest than that: to simply share what was important to me in each book and to point out what I felt was the highlight of each one. I've also included three of my own books, not just out of vanity but because feedback from hundreds of readers each year has convinced me they've got something to offer other writers. I have included website or blog addresses when available and relevant.

*Bird by Bird: Some Instructions on Writing and Life*, by Anne Lamott, Pantheon Books, 1994. This book is as instructive as it is entertaining, by a bestselling author of both fiction and nonfiction. Through anecdotes and often humorous reflections on her own life as an author, Lamott provides a clear picture of how the creative process emerges from our own life experience. She offers some of the most down-to-earth advice about writing that I've ever read — covering everything from crafting dialogue to choosing the right person to give you feedback on your first drafts. (Nice interview of Anne at her presentation at Powell's Books in Portland, Oregon: www.powells.com/authors/lamott.html)

*Courage and Craft: Writing Your Life into Story.* by Barbara Abercrombie, New World Library, 2007. As the title of this book suggests, this book is about finding the courage (and, I might add, the tenacity) to write a memoir or autobiography. But I also found it invaluable for confronting the demons that keep us from excavating our own lives for the truths that make any kind of writing worth the struggle. The book is designed like a writing course, with exercises to get you going and keep you writing. Visit her blog at this address: http://writingtime.typepad.com

*Creating Unforgettable Characters*: *A Practical Guide to Character Development*, by Linda Seger, Henry Holt, 1990. For beginning or accomplished writers, this book delves deeply into all the aspects of creating believable and compelling characters for novels, short stories, creative nonfiction, film, and TV. The author goes way beyond craft to explore issues such as psychological credibility and making the unbelievable believable. Website: www.lindaseger.com/index.html

*Creative Nonfiction*, edited by Carolyn Forché and Philip Gerard, Story Press, 2001. Thirty-plus essays on creative nonfiction, including one by Phillip Lopate on building yourself as character, one by Terry Tempest Williams on looking at your own reasons for writing, and a bizarre little story by Barry Lopez, which beautifully illustrates the creative nonfiction form, of the time he was propositioned by a woman to kill her husband. (No, he didn't do it — at least, that's what he says.) This anthology of creative nonfiction essays, some of them about the form, some exemplifying the form, is a good place to start exploring this popular literary form that blends the techniques of fiction and nonfiction. Website is for the Associated Writing Programs, whose teachers were all contributors to this book: www.awpwriter.org

*Finding Your Writer's Voice: A Guide to Creative Fiction*, by Thaisa Frank and Dorothy Wall, St. Martin's Press, 1994. This book takes a lot of the unnecessary "mystery" out of finding your own voice as a writer. The authors provide writing exercises that allow you to drop right into your own most authentic voice. The lesson this book offers seems obvious after the fact: that we don't invent our true voice nor do we have to search outside ourselves for it. It comes from within, forged from our own life experience.

*Free Play: Improvisation in Life and Art*, by Stephen Nachmanovitch, Tarcher/Putnam, 1990. Take a journey with this author into the deep creative consciousness that starts with play. This one quote from the book gives you a taste: "The child we were and are learns by exploring and experimenting, insistently snooping into every little corner that is open to us — and into the

199

forbidden corners too!" The author helps us remember the richness of play in our own lives and reclaim it in the creative process. Website: www.freeplay.com

*Henry Miller on Writing*, edited by Thomas H. Moore, New Directions, 1964. Selected writings of Henry Miller on the challenges of becoming a writer — and a self-taught one at that. The book is in four parts: The "Literary" Writer; Finding His Own Voice; The Author at Work; and Writing and Obscenity. Whether you're a Henry Miller fan or you're exploring relationships between life and the creative process, you'll find this a lively and informative read. Here's a wonderful website paying tribute to Henry, by his daughter Valentine: www.henry miller.info

*How to Write a Damn Good Novel: A Step-by-Step No Nonsense Guide to Dramatic Storytelling*, by James N. Frey, St. Martin's Press, 1987. This book has become a classic, sage advice for anyone wanting to write a popular novel. I read it once or twice a year, for the lively style and illustrative excerpts from some of the world's greatest novels. There's a *How to Write a Damn Good Novel I* and *II*. Read them both. Website: www.jamesnfrey.com

*How to Write with a Collaborator*, by Hal Zina Bennett and Michael Larsen, Authors Guild Back in Print Editions/iUniverse, 2004. Everything you need to know to collaborate with another author or become a ghost writer. What few people outside the publishing industry know is that a huge number of the bestselling authors work with other writers to develop their books. True in both fiction and nonfiction. A great way to break into publishing and build a career as a professional writer. Website: www.halzinabennett.com

*Master Plots...And How to Build Them*, by Ronald B. Tobias, Writers Digest Books, 1993. Tells how to use plot to integrate all elements of a story. The author explores twenty master plots: quest; adventure; pursuit; rescue; escape; revenge; the riddle; rivalry; underdog; temptation; metamorphosis; transformation; maturation; love; forbidden love; sacrifice; discovery; wretched excess; ascension; and descension.

*Memoirs of the Soul: A Writing Guide*, by Nan Phifer, Ingot Press, 2009. This is a real nuts-and-bolts approach to writing personal memoirs, providing clear and simple instructions that will get you started and keep you writing. The author describes twenty-two poignant life themes and experiences, with hints on how best to write them. While not formulaic in her approach, Phifer provides such clear guidelines and support that even beginners will feel confident that they can write a memoir that readers will thoroughly enjoy. Website: www.memoirworkshops.com

*Mindmapping: Your Personal Guide to Exploring Creativity and Problem-Solving*, by Joyce Wycoff, Berkeley Books, 1991. I tell my students that a book is a three-dimensional construction that cannot be organized by simple linear outlines. Mindmapping is an ingenious process for using the human brain's holographic and multidimensional capacities to the fullest. If you're an intuitive thinker, you'll catch on quickly; if you're more linear in your thinking, mindmapping can be a challenge. Either way, mindmapping should be in every serious writer's toolkit. This website includes a download for mindmapping software by the inventor of the system, Tony Buzan: www.imindmap.com

*Negotiating with the Dead: A Writer on Writing*, by Margaret Atwood, Anchor Books, 2002. Author Terrence McKenna — one of the foremost explorers of the inner landscape of human consciousness — often said that "the world is made of language." That's an unsolvable puzzle that every writer takes on every time she or he puts pen to paper. In this classic by Margaret Atwood, we meet a good partner in the exploration of that puzzle.

*Standing at Water's Edge: Moving Past Fear, Blocks, and Pitfalls to Discover the Power of Creative Immersion*, by Anne Paris, PhD, New World Library, 2008. Though the author's intended readers seem to be other psychotherapists, this is an important book for writers as well. I particularly applaud her research into the human need for connectedness that we satisfy in "creative immersion." It's something we find in every great writer's work — and every writer should consider it part of the craft. Website includes links to interviews: www.anneparis.com

*Story: Substance, Structure, Style, and the Principles of Screenwriting,* by Robert McKee, Regan Books/Harper Collins, 1997. I included this book on my list both because so many people are interested in screenwriting and because the author's wisdom about form is without parallel. McKee is recognized as the master teacher of screenwriting whose students have taken hundreds of awards for film scripts they have written. Fascinating reading, with examples drawn from hundreds of award-winning films. Website: www.mckeestory.com

*Storycatcher: Making Sense of Our Lives Through the Power and Practice of Story,* by Christina Baldwin, New World Library, 2005. Christina has a profound understanding of the relationship among language, community, intimacy, and storytelling. From her earlier classic, *Life's Companion,* to this one, she's always merged form and function in a way that creates deep understanding. This is an important book for both writers and readers. Read it slowly... and don't understand it too quickly. Website: www.storycatcher.net

*Write from the Heart: Unleashing the Power of Your Creativity,* by Hal Zina Bennett, New World Library, 1995, 2001. In a personal letter to me, a reader described this book as "an especially good guide for those wondering where their stories really begin." That's what I'd intended in writing it, offering a way of accessing the peak experiences of our lives, where we find the themes and passions that make our words lift off the page. Website: www.halzinabennett.com

*Writing Spiritual Books: A Bestselling Writer's Guide to Successful Publication*, by Hal Zina Bennett, Inner Ocean/New World Library, 2004. This book explores the unique challenges of reaching readers who are opening themselves to the deeply affecting subject matter of greater awareness and personal change. Books in these genres reach into some very tender and vulnerable parts of their readers, requiring care, honesty, and compassion not always necessary with other genres. The book covers a broad range of subjects, from writing techniques to finding the right agent, publisher, and even bookstore to handle your finished writing. Website: www.halzinabennett.com

# Internet Resources for Writers

www.AARonline.org

This is the website for the Association of Authors' Representatives (AAR). It describes what the organization does and offers a searchable database of their members. Website addresses of agents are listed so that you can track down exactly the right agent for you. There's also a good FAQ section telling what to expect of a good agent.

www.AgentQuery.com

This is a website every writer should bookmark and visit often. It's mainly a searchable database for finding literary agents but also offers clearly written articles on everything from writing a good query letter to finding a good publisher.

www.AgentResearch.com

Agent Research & Evaluation keeps an up-to-date database of reputable literary agents and is a watchdog for scams. While basic info is free, they have a fee-based service for matching you up with just the right agent. Check it out. They're definitely for real and their insider's view of the business is invaluable.

www.BabyNameWizard.com

Need to brainstorm names for your characters? The lists provided here tell about the names' origins, which can be important if, for example, you're writing a book about a certain time in history or a specific ethnic background. You'll have to put up with some really annoying ads, but the information on names is excellent.

www.Bartleby.com

This is a great resource for finding quotes from literature and to read even quite long sections of books that are — I believe — mostly in the public domain. I tried looking up a couple of T. S. Eliot quotes here, from three- and four-word portions of his work that I had remembered. It worked great. Explore this site. It'll be well worth your time.

www.BooksAndTales.com/pod/index.php

Books and Tales is a good place to begin exploring self-publishing and print-on-demand (POD) publishing. They compare POD publishers, their services, their prices, and how to find the publishers' own websites. There's also a forum for authors who've used the services listed. The pricing listed for the publishers isn't always current, however.

www.Canteach.ca/elementary/prompts.html

This website is intended for teachers. The prompts offered are pretty rudimentary, with suggestions for topics to write about, such as, "What is the best way to treat meddlesome people?" Print out a long list of one-line prompts that are good for getting you writing when you don't want to get into something more demanding.

www.Copyright.gov

Most writers eventually have questions about copyright — when and why and how to protect your work. This site not only has all the answers in its FAQ section but also provides forms and addresses for submitting your material for copyright.

www.FundsForWriters.com

Grants, contests, markets, and newsletters for writers, edited by C. Hope Clark. Where to search databases for writing grants, contests, and markets (literary journals and publishers), as well as to subscribe to newsletters. Website includes links to dozens of other websites for writers.

www.GrammarBook.com

Great place to go for all your questions about grammar and punctuation. Includes a handy FAQ list and referrals to excellent grammar books. I found the search function worked well as long as you used the exact spelling of what you were looking for. The site offers relevant resources such as books, other websites, and free lists of grammar tips.

www.ipl.org/div/farq

This is the website for "The Internet Public Library." Hosted by the University of Michigan, it's like having your own reference librarian at your beck and call. This is another of those websites that writers should spend some time exploring — and it's definitely one to bookmark on your browser.

www.NathanBransford.Blogspot.Com

Hundreds of literary agents have websites, but most provide little more than submission guidelines and a sampling of their clients' books. This one offers generous information, with glimpses into what agents do and what they want from authors. Bransford does all this with humor and style. Go here to get acquainted with the world of literary agents.

www.PlanetSARK.com

Ignite your imagination! This is arguably the internet's most colorful, original, resource-rich website there is, for writers, artists, and other creative folks. Any time you're in need of inspiration, whimsy, and subtle wisdom, come here ready to play. There's a free eletter you can subscribe to, a creative community you can join, and free online resources to download. Consult with SARK's cat Jupiter, a furry oracle of sorts! SARK's wonderful books have inspired the souls of writers and artists for years. Here's a partial list: *Eat Mangoes Naked*, *SARK's New Creative Companion*, *Make Your Creative Dreams Real*, and *Juicy Pens, Thirsty Paper*.

www.ScriptwritersNetwork.org

The Scriptwriters Network is a nonprofit, volunteer-based organization of writers helping writers. Founded in 1986, it has regular meetings to inform members about the realities of the business, to provide access to industry professionals, and to further the quality of scriptwriting. Website has informative articles. Annual membership fee.

www.ShawGuides.com

Are you looking for a writers' workshop or conference — or any kind of workshop, for that matter? Shaw-Guides has been around for a long time; they have a comprehensive database that's searchable by several parameters: date, topic, region, and so on.

www.StoryCatcher.net

This is the website of Christina Baldwin, whose book *Life's Companion* launched journal writing as a spiritual practice in the 1970s. *Storycatcher*, her newest book, explores how storytelling helps us makes sense of our lives. Learn more about journaling and storytelling or share your own stories with a network of other "story catchers."

www.wow-WomenOnWriting.com

WOW is an active and informative website about writing and publishing from a woman's point of view. Includes a newsletter as well as regular articles by women writers, notices about contests, plus resources, classes, and blogs. Well worth a visit to this one.

www.WritingContests.wordpress.com

Interested in entering a writing contest? This is a searchable database that seems to be updated frequently.

# Acknowledgments

Long ago I learned that no book is the work of the author alone. Behind the scenes there's a team of skilled and dedicated women and men who make it happen. Though we may never meet in person, be assured that I appreciate your contribution. Thank you.

Thanks Barbara Neighbor Deals, friend and literary agent, for placing this book with my favorite publisher but also for good book talk and for special humor at exactly the right moments.

Thank you once again, Jason Gardner, my editor at New World Library. This is the second book we have worked on together and, once again, your creativity, professionalism, and understanding of the inner workings of writers have made the process of "grooming" the manuscript a pleasure.

Thanks to art director Mary Ann Casler, production director Tona Pearce Myers, copy editor Pam Suwinsky, my friend and fellow writer Jan Allegretti for "still one more proof," publicist Monique Muhlenkamp, and the many other "unsung heroes and heroines" in the front office.

Marc Allen and Munro Magruder, I am indebted to you for your enthusiastic support and for one of the more admirable publishing ventures in the business today.

Finally, and most fondly, my special thanks to the thousands of readers, students, clients, and friends who have helped me probe and better understand the inner workings of the creative process.

And always, my thanks and gratitude for Susan — wife, friend, and partner — for your love and support through both challenging and joyful times.

# About the Author

Hal Zina Bennett is the author of more than thirty successful books, including three works of fiction, a volume of poetry, and nonfiction works on human consciousness, Earth-based spirituality, health, education, and creativity. He lectures and teaches throughout the United States and online internationally. As a much-sought-after personal writing coach, he has worked with authors of several national bestsellers. In his combined roles as editor, ghostwriter, collaborator, and coach he has helped authors and publishers develop over 250 successful books.

Hal holds a PhD in psychology and an MA in holistic health sciences and is a graduate of the creative writing program at San Francisco State University.

His books are published in seven languages and his articles have appeared in many popular periodicals, including *Shaman's Drum* magazine (United States), *Sacred Hoop* (England), and *Bres* (Netherlands).

He lives on a small lake in northern California with his wife, Susan J. Sparrow, two cats, named K.C. (Kitty Cat) and Y.C. (Yellow Cat), a wild opossum named Pogo, and miscellaneous beings who have not yet officially introduced themselves. Website: www.HalZinaBennett.com

# Field Notes

Use these pages to add notes such as new books for writers that you learn about, website addresses for writers' resources, names of agents or publishers, or other resources that you want to remember.

_____

_____

_____

_____

_____

_____

_____

_____

_____

_____

_____

_____

_____

_____

NEW WORLD LIBRARY is dedicated to publishing books and other media that inspire and challenge us to improve the quality of our lives and the world.

We are a socially and environmentally aware company, and we strive to embody the ideals presented in our publications. We recognize that we have an ethical responsibility to our customers, our staff members, and our planet.

We serve our customers by creating the finest publications possible on personal growth, creativity, spirituality, wellness, and other areas of emerging importance. We serve New World Library employees with generous benefits, significant profit sharing, and constant encouragement to pursue their most expansive dreams.

As a member of the Green Press Initiative, we print an increasing number of books with soy-based ink on 100 percent postconsumer-waste recycled paper. Also, we power our offices with solar energy and contribute to nonprofit organizations working to make the world a better place for us all.

Our products are available
in bookstores everywhere.
For our catalog, please contact:

New World Library
14 Pamaron Way
Novato, California 94949

Phone: 415-884-2100 or 800-972-6657
Catalog requests: Ext. 50
Orders: Ext. 52
Fax: 415-884-2199
Email: escort@newworldlibrary.com

To subscribe to our electronic newsletter, visit
www.newworldlibrary.com

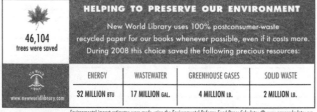

**HELPING TO PRESERVE OUR ENVIRONMENT**

46,104 trees were saved

New World Library uses 100% postconsumer-waste recycled paper for our books whenever possible, even if it costs more. During 2008 this choice saved the following precious resources:

| ENERGY | WASTEWATER | GREENHOUSE GASES | SOLID WASTE |
| --- | --- | --- | --- |
| 32 MILLION BTU | 17 MILLION GAL. | 4 MILLION LB. | 2 MILLION LB. |

Environmental impact estimates were made using the Environmental Defense Fund Paper Calculator © www.papercalculator.org.